Interview Preparation

A Simple Makeover for Anyone Preparing for a Job Interview by Having Winning Body Language

(Secrets, Tips and Techniques for Successful Interview and Get the Job)

William Haynes

Published by Rob Miles

William Haynes

All Rights Reserved

Interview Preparation: A Simple Makeover for Anyone Preparing for a Job Interview by Having Winning Body Language (Secrets, Tips and Techniques for Successful Interview and Get the Job)

ISBN 978-1-989990-77-3

All rights reserved. No part of this guide may be reproduced in any form without permission in writing from the publisher except in the case of brief quotations embodied in critical articles or reviews.

Legal & Disclaimer

The information contained in this book is not designed to replace or take the place of any form of medicine or professional medical advice. The information in this book has been provided for educational and entertainment purposes only.

The information contained in this book has been compiled from sources deemed reliable, and it is accurate to the best of the Author's knowledge; however, the Author cannot guarantee its accuracy and validity and cannot be held liable for any errors or omissions. Changes are periodically made to this book. You must consult your doctor or get professional medical advice before using any of the suggested remedies, techniques, or information in this book.

Upon using the information contained in this book, you agree to hold harmless the Author from and against any damages, costs, and expenses, including any legal fees potentially resulting from the application of any of the information provided by this guide. This disclaimer applies to any damages or injury caused by the use and application, whether directly or indirectly, of any advice or information presented, whether for breach of contract, tort, negligence, personal injury, criminal intent, or under any other cause of action.

You agree to accept all risks of using the information presented inside this book. You need to consult a professional medical practitioner in order to ensure you are both able and healthy enough to participate in this program.

Table of Contents

INTRODUCTION 1

CHAPTER 1: HOW TO LOOK FOR A JOB 3

CHAPTER 2: THE FIVE SECRETS YOU MUST KNOW TO GET HIRED 11

CHAPTER 3: 10 MOST ASKED JOB INTERVIEW QUESTIONS & ANSWERS 20

CHAPTER 4: OBJECTIVES OF INTERVIEW: 27

CHAPTER 5: MORE INTERVIEW QUESTIONS & ANSWERS! 34

CHAPTER 6: ABILITY, WILLINGNESS AND SUITABILITY (AWS) 52

CHAPTER 7: FIRST IMPRESSION 66

CHAPTER 8: DO YOUR HOMEWORK 74

CHAPTER 9: THE STRATEGY THAT IS COMMUNICATION .. 85

CHAPTER 10: PREPARING FOR QUESTIONS 90

CHAPTER 11: AFTER THE INTERVIEW 94

CHAPTER 12: HOW TO MAKE A LASTING IMPRESSION ON THE INTERVIEWERS 97

CHAPTER 13: SOFT SKILLS 100

CHAPTER 14: NEVER MAKE ASSUMPTIONS IN THE INTERVIEW 106

CHAPTER 15: EXPECTANCY OF EMPLOYERS AND THEIR TACTICS 117

CHAPTER 16: AFTER THE INTERVIEW 125

CHAPTER 17: POST INTERVIEW - SAYING "THANK YOU" 129

CHAPTER 18: PREPARING FOR THE INFORMATIONAL INTERVIEW 132

CHAPTER 19: THE #1 TECHNIQUES TO ENHANCE YOUR SUCCESS 135

CHAPTER 20: MASQUERADE – THE PHONE INTERVIEW . 138

CHAPTER 21: THE IMPORTANCE OF RESEARCH 143

CHAPTER 22: RESEARCHING THE COMPANY 149

CHAPTER 23: EMPLOYEE HYGIENE AND WELFARE 153

CHAPTER 24: OPTIMIZE YOUR RESUME 171

CHAPTER 25: AFTER THE INTERVIEW 189

CONCLUSION 198

Introduction

You've done everything you can to land that dream job; attended the best program, maybe obtained additional certificates or training, been to more networking events than you can count, memorized the names and faces of everyone at the company. Ok, maybe the last one is a bit extreme, but the point is, the moment has come to land that job. It's time for the INTERVIEW! If only there was some way to find out what potential employers want—a way to get inside their brains... WAIT, there is! That's what the **Interview Insider** is all about.

The **Interview Insider** is a peek into the minds of employers. In this book, you'll learn about the interview process from an employer's point of view. What does a "dream employee" look like? What qualifications do employers most desire in their employees? What characteristics are they looking for?

Along the way, you'll hear from leading experts. You'll also learn the silent cues interviewees send employers throughout the interview process. As well as the cues interviewers may be sending you. Finally, the **Interview Insider** will examine several pitfalls to avoid and help you unearth new language to help land the job of your dreams.

Chapter 1: How To Look For A Job

There are two types of job seekers in this world, passive and active. We, as recruiters, are always trying to find new and innovative ways to hook-line-and-sinker these passive job seekers. The reason is, they tend to be very valuable to an organization and often come with the most refined and in-demand skill-sets. A passive job seeker, as you probably guessed by the self-explanatory title, is a person who's "looking" for a job but hasn't necessarily put any "feelers" out there by filling out job applications or even posting their resume online. Instead, they might take another job and leave their current company and position, you know the one you could've had if you didn't live by the mottos, "C's equal degrees" and "Y.O.L.O." while in college, if a more enticing position was offered to them; one that required little to no effort in transitioning into or that practically fell in their lap. These passive job seekers are often referred to as "purple squirrels" in our industry. They come with just the right education, expertise, and professionalism. Their qualifications and experience have often earned them rights to establish "best practice" principals for their institutions and sometimes even their industries.

Passive job seekers rarely have to apply to jobs, because jobs are so often offered to them. In order to become a passive job seeker, instead of an active one, you must excel in whatever industry you are in. The cliché phrase is tried and true that learning is earning. So, continue learning your craft and the jobs will come to you!

By deductive reasoning, or at least, hopefully, process of elimination, you've probably figured out that an active job seeker is exactly opposite. They may come with a few expert qualities and professionalism; however, the major difference is an active job seeker is out in the job market actively looking and applying to any or everything possible to alleviate their current, or lack there of, job and financial situation. They're filling out applications, talking to friends and family about new opportunities, knocking on doors, and submitting their resume to every applicant tracking system that'll take it. If you're reading this book, chances are, you're not a passive job seeker, but instead an active one, who's decided not just to look for a job, but properly educate themself on how to get a job. You've thrown all your mottos you learned from your peers at your alma matter out the window and are finally taking the right steps in becoming a contributing member in society.

Now, obviously, the best time to look for a job is when you have a job, but if you've found yourself in the situation, like many unfortunate people have, myself included, where you are unemployed or are on the verge of facing unemployment, you've already taken the necessary course of action by reading this book. So, let's dive right in and discuss the right and wrong ways to look for a job.

We now live in a digital age. You no longer have to go door to door or even tell anyone that you're looking for a job when you're actually looking for a job. All you have to do is have a basic understanding of computers and let the Internet do all the legwork for you. Thanks to companies like CareerBuilder and Zip Recruiter, their "quick apply" approach has revolutionized the way applicants are applying for jobs now-a-days. You now have the capability to apply to 50 different jobs in less than an hour with the simple click of a button or from a smartphone in the palm of your hand while you're in the bathroom making room for dinner. You simply upload your resume, the one that you've reached out to me for to help you put together, and apply to jobs that are cross-referenced with key words in your search and on your resume. You can also request a notification to have jobs emailed to you that have certain words in their job descriptions, posted in various geographical locations. You can apply to 13 different jobs in 13 different states and/or countries simultaneously. It's borderline scary. It's to the point now, when I call an applicant, sometimes, I'm no longer surprised when they have no idea what job they've applied to or why I'm calling. This is bad. Know the jobs you're applying to and know the company that calls you. Nothing is worse than starting on an awkward foot with a hiring manager or recruiter. The odds of your recovery and job acquisition lessen by the second. If you're not familiar with the online platform of job hunting feel free to reach out to me personally via LinkedIn or signup to take one of my online courses.

If you've chosen not to go the technological route when looking for a job, but rather exponentially increase your employment opportunity costs, recruitment firms are another great resource you, as a human, have at your disposal that you may be forgetting about. Recruitment firms are basically a legal market for human trafficking, except in this scenario, everyone wins and there's no drugs, nudity, or violence involved. Recruitment firms are in the business of selling people. Sales, like everything else, you buy low and sell high. They acquire clients that are willing to pay them a particular rate in exchange for a reliable or superior employee and then turn around and hire someone to do that work for a percentage of what their client is paying them to get the job done. You, as the unemployed, accept the recruitment firm's offer, because you have no income at that particular moment and didn't find that job on your own. They buy your labor low and then sell it high to profit. All they had to do was let you find them through good marketing, and everyone's eating and making more room for dinner. Now, by law, recruitment firms have to pay you competitively and are obligated to follow minimum wage laws, just like any business, so getting a job through a recruitment firm is always a great tool to utilize. You'll be paid fairly, on time, and rarely have to worry about certain day-to-day melodramas or office politics. Recruitment firms are a reliable and free resource in saving time when interviewing at multiple places for jobs you may not want. You simply submit your resume and interview with a recruiter, or recruiters, and they go knocking on their clients' doors to get your resume in the hiring manager's hands before anyone else off the street. In fact, companies often solely go through recruiting firms when hiring in order to save time and money spent by staff interviewing these aforementioned "people off the street." A recruitment firm will only bring the best of the best applicants to a hiring manager's desk, often times passive candidates if the recruitment firm is that good, reinforcing the established business relationship and continued source of income from that client. That company will always pay that firm to find employees for them, if said employees excel and live up to expectations. If you want to receive more information on choosing a recruiting firm to work with, contact me directly via LinkedIn.

Cold calling, door-to-door, and asking friends and family are amongst the last resorts when it comes to searching for a job. Sometimes, they can pay the most, but often are the slowest and hardest to attain. When done improperly, this form of job searching can come across as desperate, unprofessional, or even unqualified. As previously stated, the best time to look for a job is when you have a job. These job-searching methods tend to have the greatest payoffs when an individual is currently employed. They may be getting terminated tomorrow, or in a week or two, but no one has to know that. The truth is, you are currently employed. With the right professionalism, you can always veil your inquisitions and appear as a passive job seeker in the eyes of the employer or friend. So, get out there and always be looking for opportunity!

Chapter 2: The Five Secrets You Must Know To Get Hired

Getting hired is the ultimate goal of all who attempt job interviews. But many people who attempt job interviews are ill prepared. I have talked to many people who have no clue as to what goes into an effective job interview preparation. Here in are revealed the secrets that should inform every preparation stage for those seeking to excel in the job interview.

There are twenty University admired key behavioral traits: they are your passport to success in any interview. Use them for reference as you customize your answers to the tough questions in the following chapters.

The Secrets Revealed

SECRET 1: Your Professional Profile is the most desirable trait to every employer. Professional traits are learned and developed as a result of our experiences in the work place.

Universally admired professional profile

All companies seek employees who respect their profession and employer. Projecting these professional traits will identify you as loyal, reliable and trustworthy.

Reliability: Following up on your-self and not relying on anyone to get the job done, and keeping management informed all the way.

Honesty / integrity: Taking responsibility for your actions, both good and bad. Always making decisions in the best interests of the co.

Pride: Pride in a job well done, always taking the extra step to make sure the job is done to the best of your ability paying attention to details.

Dedication: Whatever it takes in time and effort to see a project through to completion, on deadline.

Analytical skills: weighing pros and cons. Not jumping at the first solution that presents itself. The short – term and long – term benefits of a solution against all its possible negatives.

Listening skills: Listening and understanding, as opposed to your turn to speak.

SECRET 2: Your <u>Personal Profile</u>: The interviewer searches for your personal profile to determine what type of person you really are.

Universally admired personality traits

The presence of these keys in your answers tells the company rep how you feel about yourself. Your chosen career and what you would be like to work with.

The following words and phrases are those you will project as part of your successful, personal profile.

Drive: A desire to get things done. Goal-oriented.

Motivation: Enthusiasm and a willingness to ask questions. A motivated person accepts challenges and does that little bit extra on every job.

Communication skills: The ability to talk and write effectively to people at all levels in a company is key to success.

Chemistry: The Company is looking for someone who doesn't get rattled, wears a smile, is confident without self-importance, gets along with others – a team player.

Energy: Someone who gives that extra effort in the little things as well as important matters.

Determination: Someone who doesn't back off when things get tough.

Confidence: Poise, friendly, honest and open to employees high or low. Not intimidated by the big brother, nor overly familiar.

SECRET 3: Your Achievement Profile: Companies have limited interests: making money, saving money and saving time, projecting your achievement profile, in however humble fashion, is the key to winning any job.

Universally admired achievement profile

Companies have limited interests: making money, saving money and saving time, projecting your achievement profile, in however humble fashion, is the key to winning any job.

Money saved: Every penny saved by your thought and efficiency is a penny earned for the company.

Time saved: Every moment served by your thought and efficiency enables your company to save money and make more in the additional time available. Double bonus.

Money earned: Generating revenue is the goal of every company.

SECRET 4: Your <u>Business profile</u>. I am determined on its own doesn't hold enough salt. It's forgotten by the interviewer the moment you utter it. Projecting your business profile is important on those occasions whereby you cannot demonstrate ways you have made money, saved money, or saved time for previous employers.

Universally admired business profile

These keys demonstrate you are always on the lookout for opportunities to contribute, and that you keep your boss informed when an opportunity arises.

***Efficiency*:** Always keeping an eye open for wastage of time, effort, resources and money.

***Economy*:** most problems have two solutions an expensive one, and one the co would prefer to implement.

Procedures: Procedures exist to keep a co profitable. Don't work around them. Means keeping your boss informed. Follow the chain of command.

Profit: All the above traits are admired because in the business world they mean profit.

Secret 5: Every one hires for the same job. No one in the history of industry and commerce has ever been added to the pay roll for the love of mankind. Regardless of the Job or Profession, we are all <u>problem solvers</u>. That's the first job description for anyone who has ever been hired for any Job, at any level of organization anywhere in the world.

This fifth secret is crucial to any Job interview and career success in any field.

Think of your profession in terms of its problem solving responsibilities.

Once you have identified the particular problem solving business you are in, you have gone a long way toward isolating what the interviewer will want to talk to you about.

Identify and list for yourself the typical problems you tackle for employers on a daily basis. Come up with plenty of specific examples. Then move on to the biggest and dirtiest problems you've been faced with Again recall specifically how you solved the problem.

Here's a technique used by corporate out placement professionals to help people develop examples of their problem – solving skills and the resultant achievements.

a) **State the problem:** what was the situation? Was it typical of your Job, or had something gone wrong? Be cautious of appointing blame.

b) **Isolate relevant background information:** what specific knowledge or education were you armed with to tackle this dilemma?

c) **List your key qualities:** What professional skills and personal behavior traits did you bring in to play to solve the problem?

d) **Recall the solution.** How did things turn out in the end? (If the problem did not have a successful resolution, do not use it as an example)

e) **Determine what the solution was worth:** Quantify the solution in terms of the money earned, money served, or time served. Specify your role as a team member or as a lone gun, as the facts demand.

If you follow the steps above, you will develop a series of Illustrative stories for each key area; remember stories help interviewers visualize you solving their problems as a paid member of the team.

We get two very special benefits when we understand and apply the fifth secret. First we show that we possess the problem solving abilities, second, when we ask about the problems, challenges, projects, deadlines and pressure points that will be tackled in the early months, we show that we will be able to hit the ground running on those first critical projects.

Chapter 3: 10 Most Asked Job Interview Questions & Answers

Describe yourself in one sentence
Tips: The best way to answer this question is to be honest and very clear in your head. Since you are limited to just one sentence, try to say something that would catch the employer's attention. You cannot brag about your education and brilliant work history in such a short space. What you can do is come up with one line to emphasize your personality, your aim and show your compatibility with the job. Following answer could be applicable to software developers etc.

Answer: I am very detail oriented and can focus on multiple tasks at a time with precision.

Tell me how you handled a difficult situation in your past
Tips: The interviewer is assessing whether you are capable of handling tough situations and what creative solutions you can come up with. Your words should

sound positive and try to come up with a situation that really was difficult to handle. You should sound like a winner who had overcome the problem situation with great ease. This should sound more like a team effort where you played the main role. Preferably narrate a professional experience if there is any.

Answer: I remember this one incident when our system had generated faulty requests against mobile numbers which could have disconnected thousands of these numbers from our network. This had to be dealt immediately. Taking control of the situation, I called an emergency team meeting and decided not to go back home till the issue is resolved. Blah blah.

How was your experience with your previous boss?

Tips Do not bad mouth your previous employer, no matter what. This sends wrong vibes to the interviewer. Why insecure him? Even if things did not work out between you and your ex-boss or ex-colleague, you should speak about them with respect and politeness in your tone.

Answer: Mr. XYZ is the most inspiring boss to work with. His working style is very motivating and encouraging. I have worked with him for three years and found him to be a man of his word. I have great respect for him deep in my heart.

Are you a good team player?

Tips Of course you are. Nobody would want to hire you otherwise. The interviewer actually wants to assess your interpersonal skills. Narrating an incident where you came to a compromise with a colleague who was creating conflict within a team would be perfect.

Answer: I remember when we were being trained for our first market experience one of my team mates was consistently asking questions that made no sense. He was not only wasting time but was also frustrating the other team members who were eagerly trying to concentrate on the training. I asked the trainers to conduct some team building games and after some time I found that the troublesome colleague of mine was actually helping out others! My trick had worked and his mind was taken off from asking nonsensical questions.

Are you looking somewhere else for job too?

Tips The interviewer is trying to evaluate how much in demand you actually are. Your line of interest also shows in your selection of job positions and organizations that you share with your interviewer. Name a few good reputable companies where you had recently applied.

Answer: I have applied for the position of Quality Assurance Manager in XYZ, blah blah.

How did you deal with a colleague you did not like?

Tips This sort of question is used to judge the interviewee's potential as a team player and the ability to resolve conflicts. It also shows your diplomatic skills as well. Choosing the right words, you can easily answer this question making a good impression on the interviewer.

Answer: I have worked with a person whom I did not like very much as a person yet I appreciated him for his knowledge and superb logical skills. These attributes were not only helpful to him but were also very useful for the other colleagues. I started growing respect for him because of this and from then on we had a nice working relationship.

Explain what you did in your last job. What were your major job responsibilities?

Tips: The interviewer is now interested in your technical/ work relevant skills. Your past experience should support the future role that you are trying to pursue. Like if you supervised a team, you could apply for a managerial post as you have experience of team leading.

Answer: I have worked for the past three years in Warid Telecom as an MNP Supervisor. My major job responsibilities were blah blah

Are you good at dealing with stress of work?

Tips: Try and answer this question as if you take stressful situations most stimulating and motivating. Stress should make you work better towards your goals than would do normally.

Answer: It depends on the situation. Hardly any situation becomes stressful to me but sometimes when it does; it tends to do more good than harm by bringing out the best in me. I can easily say that it helps me excel even more under pressure. Then managing my work properly and working out after work helps me deal with any unnecessary pressure.

Can you put company's interest ahead of you?

Tips: The only answer to this question is yes. You cannot answer otherwise since it portrays a bad picture of you. Nobody wants to hire a person who gives them lower priority than others.

Answer: Yes, my company's priorities are most important to me than anything.

What makes you think you are best suited for this job?

Tips: Your answer should not sound boring as if reading out a sample answer taken from a website. Rather be creative and honest. Answer by providing all your excellent skills and experience that has relevance to your job. You ARE the best candidate. Now go on and prove it to the interviewer.

Answer: My past experience and relevant educational background allows me to say that I am definitely the best candidate for this job. My excellent skills in this field enable me to offer my very best services and to add valuable contribution to your company.

Chapter 4: Objectives Of Interview:

It helps to verify the information provided by the candidate. It helps to ascertain the accuracy of the provided facts and information about the candidate.

What the candidate has written in the resume are the main points. What other additional skill set does he have? All these are known by conducting interviews.

It not only gives the interviewer information about the candidate's technical knowledge but also gives an insight into his much needed creative and analytical skills.

It helps in establishing a mutual relation between the employee and the company.

It is useful for the candidate so that he comes to know about his profession, the type of work that is expected from him, and he gets to know about the company.

It is beneficial for the interviewer and the interviewee as individuals, because both of them gain experience, both professionally and personally.

It helps the candidate assess his skills and knows where he lacks and the places where he needs improvement.

It also helps the company build its credentials and image among the employment seeking candidates.

In the current job market, you'd better have your act together, or you won't stand a chance against the competition. Be prepared to the best of your ability. There is no way to predict what an interview holds, but by following these important rules, you will feel less anxious and will be ready to positively present yourself. Check yourself on these basic points before you go on that all-important interview

Do your research

Researching the company before the interview and learning, however much as could be expected about its administrations, items, clients, and rivalry will give you an edge in comprehension and tending to the company's needs. The more you think about the company and a big motivator for it, the better possibility you have of selling yourself in the interview. You additionally should get some answers concerning the company's way of life to pick up an understanding of your potential satisfaction at work. You ought to have the option to discover a great deal of data about the company's history, crucial qualities, staff, culture, and ongoing victories on its site. On the off chance that the company has a blog and a web-based life nearness, they can be valuable spots to look, as well

Dress sharp

Try not to hold up until the last moment to choose an interview outfit, print additional duplicates of your resume, or discover a notebook and pen. Have one great interview outfit prepared, so you can interview without prior warning stressing over what to wear. At the point when you have an interview arranged, prepare everything the prior night.

Not exclusively will arranging out everything (from what shoes you will wear, to how you'll style your hair, to what time you will leave and how you'll arrive) get you time toward the beginning of the day, it can help lessen pursuit of employment uneasiness, and it will likewise spare you from deciding, which means you can utilize that intellectual prowess for your interview. Ensure your interview clothing is slick, clean, and fitting for the sort of firm you are interviewing with. Carry a pleasant portfolio with additional duplicates of your resume. Incorporate a pen and paper for note-taking.

Be punctual

Be on time for the interview. On-time means five to ten minutes early. If need be, drive to the interview location ahead of time, so you know exactly where you are going and how long it will take to get there. Take into account the time of your interview so you can adjust for local traffic patterns at that time. Give yourself a few extra minutes to visit the restroom, check your outfit, and calm your nerves.

Make your selling points clear

If a tree falls in the forest and no one is there to hear it, did it make a sound? More important, if you communicate your selling points during a job interview and the interviewer doesn't get it, did you score? On this question, the answer is clear: No! So don't bury your selling points in long-winded stories. Instead, tell the interviewer what your selling point is first, then give the example.

Speak the right body language

Dress appropriately, make eye contact, give a firm handshake, have good posture, speak clearly, and don't wear perfume or cologne! Sometimes interview locations are small rooms that may lack good air circulation. You want the interviewer paying attention to your job qualifications -- not passing out because you've come in wearing Malizia and the candidate before you were doused with Brut, and the two have mixed to form a poisonous gas that results in you not getting an offer.

Be Succinct (and Definitely, Don't Recite Your Resume)

Whatever you do, don't waste this time regurgitating every single detail of your career. Most people answer it like they're giving a dissertation on their resume, but that's only going to bore the interviewer to tears.

There's no deductively demonstrated ideal length for noting this or any interview question. A few mentors and spotters will guide you to hold it to 30 seconds or less, while others will say you should go for a moment, or talk for close to two minutes. Be that as it may, in his experience, individuals will in general, start losing steam after 1.5 to 2.5 minutes of continuous talking. You'll need to choose what feels directly for you in some random setting, yet in case you're representing longer than a few minutes, there's a decent possibility you're diving into an excess of detail too early. Ensure you're additionally perusing the room as you're talking. In the event that the other individual looks exhausted or diverted, it may be an ideal opportunity to wrap it up. On the off chance that they liven up at one piece of your answer, it may merit developing that point more.

Follow-Up After the Interview

Always follow up with a thank-you note reiterating your interest in the position. You can also include any details you may have forgotten to mention during your interview. If you interview with multiple people from the same company, send each one a personal note. Send your thank-you email within 24 hours of your interview.

Chapter 5: More Interview Questions & Answers!

"Fall seven times, stand up eight."——Japanese proverb

You can never get enough of practicing answers to tricky questions that could creep up during the interview. The first thing you should try to do after an interview is to sit and re-evaluate the questions you were asked and your responses. Record your meeting at any interview location. There are various downloadable apps that can help you with that and if you'd prefer not to use a Smartphone you could easily get a voice recorder for that purpose. Be sure to keep it hidden discreetly though, not everyone would be comfortable with the idea of you recording an interview even if there's no explicit law against it. Reviewing your past interviews will help you know what to work on in subsequent interview sessions. That's why I've thought it best that I should add more of the most common questions that you'll be asked during interviews across any career path. The questions might differ slightly in wording from interview to interview but the motivations behind them still remain the same. The aim is to find out what you bring to the table in regards to taking the company to greater heights. Here are some more questions and answers you're likely to come cross in one interview or the other. According to online career site Glassdor.com these are some of the most common interview questions in 2014. We'll start with the most expected yet the most dreaded question.

What are your weaknesses?

This is a very clichéd question now but it still does a great job of tripping up a lot of prospective employees. The question might also be asked in other ways like; what would your former managers have liked you to improve on? Many interviewees have one clichéd answer to this. "I'm a perfectionist" Well that might have done the job a few decades ago but it won't do the job now. Hiring managers have heard this answer so many times; they'd really appreciate more originality.

A more believable strategy would be to pick out a weakness you're working on and highlight what steps you're making to resolve it and how much progress you've made. You could say

"My duties used to keep me in the house a lot and cut off any chances I had of having a healthy social life. I never thought much of it at first but I soon realized I couldn't be at my best without a healthy balance in life. Now I make it a point to take little breaks in between my work hours and on weekends I now engage in more outdoor activities. Specifically I now love kayaking and I actively participate at my local indoor rock climbing club. Surprisingly, it's not affected my work output like I used to think it might. It's actually made me much more productive."

We all have some weaknesses and not admitting our weakness to the interviewer will give an impression of being untruthful and maybe arrogant.

If you're going to use a personal weakness as an answer to this question, make sure it's related to the job position you're angling to secure. If it doesn't match then it could backfire on you.

What are your strengths?

This question is an open invitation to sell yourself and your relevant skills on the job to your interviewer. It's time to go back to the list of strengths everyone should sit down to write a couple of days before any interview. It could be anything related to the job that stands you out above average from among the mass of other competing candidates. Like any other question in the interview, your strengths will be more believable to the interviewer if you have real-life scenarios to back up your points.

Where do you see yourself five years from now?

Here's a trick question if you'll ever see one. It's designed to find out if the company fits into your long term plans. The interviewer wants to know if your commitment level and ambitions are favorably aligned with the organization.

Give an answer that reflects your commitment to career improvement, probably highlighting a specific area of your duties you'd like to acquire more expertise. You could give an answer like this:

"In 5 years I see myself having a deeper knowledge of the industry and taking up the responsibility of training a team that is better equipped to handle challenging situations. I particularly see myself becoming an expert at SQL and SAAS programming as I've always had a particular interest in those areas. "

Why did you leave /or do you want to leave your last job?

Be wary of this question, the interviewer is very aware that whatever you say about your previous or present employer- whichever it might be- will also be something you're likely to say about this organization. Do not make the mistake of being drawn in on speaking negatively of the culture, internal politics or financial benefits of your employer. All that will be seen as negative. Stay away from speaking negatively about your duties as well, especially if you're not sure of all the duties that might be assigned to you in this new position. It's best to play it safe. In response to the question you might say something like:

"There wasn't anything in my last job that I hated; but I obviously didn't like some aspects as much as I loved others. My present job requires me to do a lot of travelling outside the state and while I do like to travel sometimes the frequency at which I am required to do so is a bit exhausting. I was required to travel at least once a week, I'm now looking to be a bit more settled."

Why was there a gap in your employment between this date and that date specified on your resume?

This is a question that most people dread. There are not too many correct ways to answer this question. It might be a good thing to highlight any programs, certifications or added skills you might have gained during the period in question. The important thing is to demonstrate you have used that period to better your career and are more equipped to take on fresh challenges - better if it is specific to the one in question - than you were before. When asked that question you could say:

"I felt I needed to go in a new direction in my career so I took a couple of years off to develop my analytical skills and recharge. I'm also very careful now with the opportunities that I target because I'm looking for specific duties like those available here."

What are your most important accomplishments?

Here's another opportunity to speak about the specifics of what you have done in your past places of employment. Detail is important, when the interviewer asks this question, he /she wants to hear a story about how you've provided value at a previous job. This is not the time to talk about when you built your house or graduated from college. If you helped your company save time or increase productivity, here's where to give details of how you did so. Be careful to give some credit to any team members you might have worked with in the process.

Can you handle Pressure?

No interviewer is going to be satisfied with only a "yes" on this question. Of course anyone will say yes, no one in their right minds will respond to that question with a "no." Explain how you delivered on your objectives despite having to work your way around various obstacles as well as an ominously ticking clock. It would also be useful to mention your habit of planning ahead of time. Not every interviewer will be convinced by your claims of being able to work under pressure.

When were you most satisfied at your Job?

Think about a specific situation where you genuinely felt the happiest on your job. It would be particularly great if there were similar opportunities being offered in the role being interviewed for. This is a chance to portray yourself as an enthusiastic individual who takes great pleasure in a job or role. No hiring manager wants an employee who finds no joy or passion in anything they.do. Saying you enjoy it all doesn't sound believable. It's necessary to. Specify something and speak with genuine passion about it. You could say:

"I love working behind the computer on lines of code and all that while solving problems but I get the most enjoyment from my job when I actually interact with people. I'm a people person and it always gives me a huge boost when 'm speaking with clients one on one."

Could you describe a time when you had a dispute with a co-worker and explain how it was resolved.

Whatever you do, never reply I get along with everyone perfectly well. No one will ever believe you even if you're being truthful. The best way to satisfactorily answer this question is to think of an instance and use it to showcase your patience and people skills. The occasion has to end on a sound note. Here's an example:

"There was this particular colleague on my team who seemed to disagree with me on everything we ever had to work on together. We always had different ideas on everything and it was hard to ever move forward on anything we had together. After over a month of butting heads over every issue, I decided I'd had enough and we couldn't continue allowing our personal differences get in the way of team productivity. I invited her out to lunch where we had the opportunity to talk about our differences in a les tense atmosphere. I was pleasantly surprised to find we had a lot of things in common and we soon began to find common ground on a lot of issues. Since then I've had the belief that no one is actually as bad as they seem as soon as you really get to know them.'

What motivates you to give your best efforts on the job?

What ever you do never make any references to being inspired by the generous salary, unusual benefits, or limitless company credit cards. Interviewers don't like to know you're only inspired by the payout they have to offer.

Make your interviewer realize that the greatest reward for you would be the satisfaction of meeting targets and even surpassing the expected results. Explain that your drive and passion for doing the best job possible are your biggest motivations.

What have you done that shows an ability to take initiative?

In this question you're expected to describe a scenario where you are involved in a team, you step up, take charge and direct affairs for the good of the team. The question expects you to show leadership qualities to take a team towards the given objective without flouting any rules or standard protocol.

How would your friends describe you?

As much as you might be tempted, this question isn't designed to give you the opportunity to describe how "cool" and how much of a people person you are. One simple rule of thumb to watch about interviews is that it's all about the job and what you can bring to the table; it's never about you. The answer to this question needs to reflect that perspective. In answer to that question you could say:

"My friends would probably say I'm very persistent when it comes to getting tasks accomplished. When I was once asked to coordinate the organization of an event, I had to get several keynote speakers to commit to attending the event. I received many rejections initially but I was persistent and wouldn't accept no for an answer. I eventually got all but one of the initial invitees to attend. No one thought I could get half of our targets to make an appearance."

What motivates you on the Job?

This question is somewhat similar to "what do you like about your last job?" It's a test of your passion for what you do for a living. Like I wrote earlier, don't give a generic response. Take your time to elaborate on your career passions. Take advantage of the opportunity and give the interviewer some insight into aspects of your personality that are both relevant to the job and endearing at the same time. A good answer to the question would be something like:

"I've always relished the challenge of a looming deadline. There's something that just pushes me to crank out that little bit of extra effort to cross the finish line ahead of time while doing a fantastic job at the same time. I know this job is very demanding, but I can hardly wait to take on the challenge."

How long have you been looking for a job?

Now this is a trick question if there ever was one. It's easy to just blurt out 3 years but that will not be to your advantage. Even if you've remained unemployed for 6 years, take into consideration all the activities you've undertaken during that time. Consider running your own business, volunteer activities, internships, consulting, studying for a certification or working for your favorite charities anything to show you have been gaining experience, adding to your skill-set and have not been idle. Subtract the time you've spent on these activities from the last time you were employed. This will make the idle period much shorter and much more attractive to a potential employer. There will be less worry about your ability to successfully re-integrate into a work environment.

Why were you fired?

As much as you might be uncomfortable answering this question if you've been fired before, it's an issue that will have to be addressed at some point or the other. It's always better to be ready for it when it comes. If you were fired as a result of your own doing, then it's up to you to try and portray the situation in the most positive way as possible. You'll also want to stress on how you've rectified the situation and grown from that into a more skilled and mature professional. Mention the references that will be willing to speak on your behalf. The task isn't so difficult if you were laid off as part of a larger downsizing exercise. Point out the larger numbers of people fired if your incident was an isolated one.

Why should I hire you?

A lot of people admit that they break into a sweat when they hear this question. But there's really nothing to fear. Remember the unique selling points you wrote about yourself before coming for the interview? Well, here's where you start to list them and convince the interviewer he'd be missing out on something huge by not offering you the job. A great answer to that question would be something similar to this:

"I've been a project management professional for 12 years now and my boss has always held me in high regard when it comes to handling duties at my organization. There are numerous times he's told me I'm the glue holding the team together and keeping the organization in business. He's always had the confidence to entrust me with vital assignments that he'd never give to anyone else. There was a time when we were 5 days behind schedule on a crucial project, he handed the project to me at that point because he felt I was the only one that could get it done. I've never been happier to complete a project than I was at that time because I was so pleased that I didn't let him down.

Why do you want this Job?

This is one of the most mind-twisting questions an interviewer might ask. Like most other questions this is a tricky one that has to be handled with care. obviously, most people really want a new job because it pays a lot more than their previous jobs or it's closer to their homes but you don't want to let the prospective employer know that. Every employer wants a deeper commitment from their employees than the paycheck or a simple matter of convenience. Here's a list of no-no answers for this one.

I have a new baby on the way.....

Cute and all but that won't cut it, there will be no jobs handed out based on sentiment.

I hate my current job.....

What's the guarantee you're not going to hate this new one after a few months? No employer wants to deal with that.

I'm a bit bored....

Being bored with your job is unprofessional and if you're bored you probably have no business being in that profession anyway.

These answers in themselves might be true, at least from your perspective but it does not state why the employer should give you the job. After all, you're not the only one who has a valid reason for applying for the position. Whoever is going to stand out from the crowd and get the job has to be the one with a compelling reason that convinces the employer that it will be in his/her best interests to hire you.

There is a three step process to answering this question to the best of your ability.

Step 1:

Exercise your powers of subtle flattery here, tell the interviewer how much you want to work in that organization and what exactly you would cherish about working there.

Step 2: Here's where you showcase the detailed understanding of what the particular position entails, you'll need to know the details of the role and the peculiar challenges that come along with it. Talk about the problems and what you look forward to doing to solve the issues involved.

Step 3: Let the interviewer know things you've done in your recent work experience that are similar to the pending tasks now. peak about what you enjoy and how you enjoy tackling the problems. if there is something that might hinder your selection by the employer, go ahead and provide a logical reason to ignore any such reasons.

Chapter 6: Ability, Willingness And Suitability (Aws)

You succeed in an interview if and only if you are able to demonstrate during an interview that you are able to do the job, you are willing to do the job and you suit the company's culture. Like a fan works on electricity, your interview works on AWS.

While I will provide a more decomposed picture of all the three in the coming paragraphs for now I want you to take things in a very simple manner. Your job is to demonstrate your ability, willingness and suitability for the applied position.

Have you ever witnessed a situation where a candidate with higher potential but poor preparation fails in an interview whereas surprisingly another candidate with lower potential but better preparation gets the offer? Actually this is no surprise. I want you to very thoroughly understand one thing that the recruiters attach far more weightage to your preparation than to your potential because your preparation gives a straight and clear signal of your willingness to the recruiter. The company has enough resources to impart the ability needed for the job but it cannot impart the willingness. The outcome of an interview usually depends on how well you prepare not how good you are. When you are on job you give the willingness and the company gives the ability and it does not happen the other way.

If you are prepared you are activating that compartment of the recruiter's mind which is under pressure from different department managers to quickly hire the required talent whereas if you are unprepared you are activating an alternate compartment of the recruiter's mind which will simply avoid taking any risk by hiring a person who **"lacks willingness."**

Which compartment to activate, the choice is your's.

Ability

Ability in simple words means the possibility that you can do the job on the basis of your technical and behavioral capabilities.

There are two components of your ability that are functional component and behavioral component.

The functional component comprises of your technical knowledge needed for the job whereas the behavioral component comprises of your soft skills needed for the job. Please not that I used the word functional knowledge not the functional know-hows above.

Every company has a competency framework and you have to demonstrate that you fit into the competency framework of the company.

Since functional capability based questions are domain specific I will not be able to cover them but I will cover the behavioral competency based questions.

Recruiters frequently look for the below behavioral capabilities so make sure you demonstrate the below as practically as possible

How meeting the deadlines is a habit for you

How you manage stress

How you work under minimum supervision

How you are both an individual and team player

How you manage lengthy tasks

How your strengths can infuse in the company

Again please know that preparation is the key. Since ability based questions cover roughly fifty percent of your interview it is essential that that you pick up only those examples which are a close match to the job requirements. Do not forget it is a lot easier to think of the examples when you are preparing for the interview than when you are actually sitting in front of the recruiter.

Some examples of competency based questions can be

What are your greatest strength?

Please make sure to mentions only those strengths which are relevant to the job and of which you are sufficiently confident.

For example, If you are sitting in a sales interview something like the below sells well.

"My biggest strength is that I carry peak level of energy throughout the day. Do not be surprised if you find me in one corner of the city in the morning and the other by the afternoon. My peak energy has continually motivated me to keep sports an integral part of my life for over a decade now."

And in highest probability the next question will be **"Oh wow!so what sports are you interested in?"**

This is how preparedness helps you find the north in front of the recruiter.

What are your weaknesses?

Please mention only those weaknesses which are not very relevant to the job. Something like the below works

"I am a little overly obsessed about grooming and I end spending a lot of time in front of the mirror"

At one instance I had to take a telephonic interview for a sales associate position and I had very limited time. Considering the limited time I opened the telephonic interview with a straight and direct question

"What is your biggest weakness?" and what came as a reply from the other side was **"I find it a little difficult to work under pressure"** and I had no other option than to reply **"ok!I will get back to you! Though I am not entirely sure of it."** Such blunders cost you the job because you lack the capability.

What skills have you acquired recently?

Give an example of how you work under pressure.

This is just an illustrative list of questions. I have provided the below in the fourth chapter

Frequently asked interview questions

What recruiters look for and don't look for in the answers.

Good and bad memorable examples for selected questions

Please note that recruiters assigns far more weightage to the behavioral component than to the functional component. It is for this reason that in the fourth chapter of this book I have made a specific section for behavioral questions and ways to answer them including the signals that you send to your recruiters.

WILLINGNESS

Willingness for a job means given the ability do you possess the mindset or the attitude to do the job?

The reason why I said that your prepared often determines the outcome of an interview is because your level of preparedness gives a very clear signal to the recruiter of how significant the job is to you and how serious you are about the job.

How you prepare helps the interviewer gauge some of the most essential aspects of needed for the job like

If hired, how significant will the job be for you?

How seriously will you consider the job?

How will you connect with and work towards the goals of the company?

How you will stick with the company in odd times to achieve a long term fulfilling relationship?

How will you answer to the call of the duty?

True job commitment is the most fundamental quality that most companies recognize and reward. Bosses generally recognize those employees who are willing to evolve and improve with the company rather switching over.

Employees' turnover is expensive so companies want you to show some degree of loyalty to them in exchange of the benefits they offer.

When you are in an interview it is needed that you exercise some judgment before answering willingness based questions. Never ever give an impression, hint or signal that you will be doing any of the below

Looking for another job in the near future
Considering the company just as "a company", lot of which come and go
Lacking ambition about the job
Looking forward to be an entrepreneur
Avoid hard work by over-smart work

Any impression, hint or signal of any of the above will lead to straight rejection. Please make sure to internalize that you strictly refrain from indicating any of the above.

It is often found that the candidates who are better prepared for the job are more likely to show job commitment if hired. In other words your level of preparation before the job often translates into you level of commitment after the job

By the way! Dear aspiring entrepreneurs! Please go ahead and pursue your passion without wasting any time in applying for jobs. Do not stand on two boats simultaneously.

There are certain things that you need to know about willingness based questions like

These questions are asked in a little subtle manner

These questions are a little difficult to handle

Candidates often do a lot of mumbo-jumbo when these questions are thrown

These questions are pivotal and can convert a "yes" to a "no" or a "no" to a "yes" in any moment of the interview.

Recruiters scan your body language most closely when you answer these questions.

Below is an illustrative list of questions to check your willingness for the job.

Have you established what you are capable of?

If one such question is thrown on you, the recruiter looks for two things

1) Yes you have established what you could

2) There is still a scope for evolving with time

If you have good grades in your academics, or hold high attendance this is one of the best places to bring your grades or attendance in the interview. An answer like the below sells well

"Yes I believe I have established what I could and the same reflects in my average eighty-five percent score throughout academics and above ninety percent attendance. Delivering peak performance while continually striving to learn is my way of life"

How long will it be before you make a net contribution?

A company usually has a structured induction program of 4 to 6 weeks and the recruiter wants you to start performing after the induction program is over.

So you can tell **"four to six weeks"** or you can tell **"I will start performing as soon as the induction program is over"**. Please do not come out with any disproportionate number like three months or six months or one year.

If you are given this job, how long will you stay with us?

Try to avoid putting any number by telling something subjective **like "I want to build a long term fulfilling relation with the company"** if it doesn't work you can put any number between three and five. Less than three becomes too short a commitment and more than five sounds too superficial and gives an indication that you lack ambition and you want to rest in the company for too long.

I have often observed that behavior based questions shatter your confidence apart whereas they should actually not. From the recruiter's side of the table these are the questions where every other candidate comes with something sillier.

Even if you stay composed and deliver an average performance on these questions you are actually better than most of the other candidates and there is a high probability that you will succeed.

If you prepare you can actually deliver a good, great or an excellent performance.

I have seen a lot of candidates like you succeed or fail in an interview and the reason why I have developed the whirlpool tool provided in chapter six is for you to more specifically handle the willingness based questions well. When I say **"this book provides the motivational architecture to support your interview"** these are the questions where you need a support to stay composed and firmly navigate the interview towards success rather losing confidence and allowing interview to automatically navigate towards failure.

SUITABILITY

Companies look only for those people who can seamlessly fit into the organization culture and ethos.

Please note that your suitability for an organization will not give you the job thought lack of suitability can cost you the job.

While answering to a suitability based question make sure to reflect that you fit into the company's

Culture and image

Vision and Mission

Values and belief system

Please note that suitability is given higher weightage in interviews for higher positions.

One of the best ways to demonstrate your suitability for a company is to research about the company through informal channels like

Facebook Page

Twitter Page

Getting to know about the company from somebody who works in the company

A walk around the office a day before will not be a bad idea. I have observed such cases. Below are some questions that recruiters ask to check your suitability

How easily are you able to adapt into the new environment?

You can describe a change that you adapted to including the strategies if any you followed.

How do you go about getting to know your new collogues?

You can just go about saying how you naturally interact with people

Where do you see yourself in next five years?

You can express your ambitions in a structured and manner considering the job you have applied for.

Chapter 7: First Impression

I am sure we have all heard the saying that the first impression is the last one, and this is especially true of job interviews. If you cannot present yourself favorably at first glance, you are not going to have s second chance. For those who think it is acceptable to go to an interview wearing jeans and sweats, you should be aware that you have already lost the job no matter how qualified you may be. You want to use the interview as a way to secure that position and in order to do so you must dress the part—in other words "Dress to Impress" to coin the title of a book on the subject of dressing for an interview.

Even if you know that the company you are going for an interview allows casual attire for their employees, you still should go well dressed. You should never dress casually for a job interview unless you are told to do so by the company and only in cases where the interview is being held in a factory or warehouse where even business casual may be out of place. When you walk into the interview you want to make the interviewer wants to take a second look and create the impression that you will be an asset to the company.

Sometimes there may be allowance such as when you work for a company with a casual dress code and you are going for an interview immediately before or after work. In this circumstance, you want to apprise the interviewer of the situation so that it will not cast you in a negative light when you arrive. Certainly if you are going to or coming from another job you don't want to dress in a different way and cast suspicion, especially if you do not desire for your former employer to know you are seeking another position.

Regardless of the circumstances, it is never acceptable to wear clothing that is torn, dirty, wrinkled or ill-fitting to an interview. If you are coming straight from another job and your clothing has become soiled take the time to change into something else even if you have to stop at a public restroom to do so. Remember, you will not have a second chance to make an impression.

The Interview Process

Before you begin to interview for your first job, you want to understand the interview process. It is unlikely that you will only be subjected to one interview—in all likelihood, before you are hired you will interview at least two times. The first interview will be with Human Resources, and if they determine you meet the requirements of the department you will meet with the department head who is responsible for doing the hiring. Sometimes you will meet with the supervisor and the manager for three interviews. In a smaller company, all of this may be combined into one in order to make a selection quickly. You may have either two interviews while you are there, you may be asked to return or you may have an interview that includes several people at the same time.

The interview process will vary depending upon the size of the company. In some smaller companies there may not be a Human Resources department at all or they may be the ones who do the actual hiring of employees. In other companies you may actually interview with the store or department manager. Making the choice that is best for the company is always the ultimate focus, so the better you are at selling yourself during the interview, the sooner you will be able to find the job you seek.

Testing may be another part of the interview process. You usually know about this when you schedule the interview so you can plan your time accordingly. The type of testing you have to do will depend upon the position for which you are applying. Even if you are right out of college with little to no experience, you may be asked to take a skills test just to assess your level of general knowledge. For an office position this may also include a typing test and testing for knowledge with various office applications. You have to be prepared to undergo all of the necessary prerequisites if you want to be hired by any company.

If the company is seriously considering hiring you, they may require you to undergo drug and alcohol testing as well. This is not something that usually will occur until they decide they would like to hire you, but it is something you must do before they will actually make a firm offer of employment.

Time Allotments Between interviews

It is not easy to guess how much time to allow between interviews, but it is better to allow too much time than not enough. Do not assume that one to two hours plus travel time will be enough time between interviews because that is not always the case. If you are anxious to schedule as many interviews as possible, you might ask the person with whom you schedule the interview to provide more specific information about interview time.

The best way to avoid potential conflicts you should limit your interviews to no more than two a day—one in the morning and one in the afternoon with a gap of at least four to five hours between them. You do not want to over schedule and then sit fidgeting while trying to hope you will be able to make the second interview on time. You might be distracted and the interviewer will be able to sense you are trying to rush, it will also cause you to take your focus off what the interviewer is saying while you attempt to rush things along.

Topics Of Discussion

The purpose of your interview is not to find out where the interviewer went to school or what their hobby is. Even if you know each other personally, you do not discuss personal topics during your interview. That does not mean you cannot ask a couple questions or discuss one event that may be common to both of you, but you do not go into a lengthy discussion about anything not related to your job application and resume.

Time is essential for both you and the interviewer, and if she or he has another interview after yours, engaging in small talk will waste time away from another applicant. Even though you want to be the one to receive the job offer you don't want to do that by taking time away from another applicant. Even if you are the last interview of the day, there may be other important things they have to attend to, and you may cause your interviewer to have to work overtime in order to finish things that must be finished before leaving for the day.

By sticking on topics that are related to the job you are applying for such as your education and experience, you will allow the interview process to remain on professional and prevent the potential of cutting someone else's time short—or even worse, cutting yours short because you are running into someone else's time. Questions such as your education and experience are relevant to the, so you want to remain on those topics as much as possible in order to remain within the period the interviewer has set aside for you.

There are many different social media platforms you can join, but most of them are not specifically tailored for professionals. LinkedIn is the best networking site for people to promote themselves and can be a very good platform to launch your career. Not very many people know how to use LinkedIn effectively for job hunting.

LinkedIn offers a great opportunity to receive recommendations from past employers or supervisors that will increase your credibility. Upload your latest resume onto LinkedIn so people who are hiring will be able to see your credentials and they will contact you if they are interested to interview you. Put a professional looking profile picture and build a great profile. Join groups of your career interest and start commenting and adding people into your network.

Chapter 8: Do Your Homework

You've probably came across plenty of interviewing tips from your parents, friends, and colleagues. Some of those tips you may have found helpful, some you may have chosen to ignore, and some may be outdated. With the current job market and unemployment rate, it's important to master and take advantage of every opportunity to interview.

The first step to acing an interview is to do your homework. Just like preparing for a presentation or an exam – you need to practice and study until you know you are ready. You're probably asking yourself, "How do you know when I'm ready?" With preparation, practice, and knowledge, your confidence will rise. After reading and applying what this book has to offer, you will come to find out what it feels like to be ready to ace an interview.

There is only so much you can learn by reading about a position and company on their website or visiting the workplace, so it's possible that you may not feel as prepared as you would like. You can always test yourself, but it's recommended to have a friend test you. Here are a few examples of what you should be asking yourself:

1) What do you know about the company?
2) What do you know about the position?
3) What are they looking for in their ideal candidate?
4) What products/services does the company have to offer?
5) How do their products/services differ from their competition?
6) Who are their competitors?
7) What are some of the industry trends?

Yes, it may seem tedious, such as a chore that you don't want to complete, but if you really want to land that job, this step is critical. Remember, you don't get a second chance to make a first impression.

Know the Organization

There are many ways to research the company and position you will be interviewing for. Your very first step should be visiting the company's website. Read all of the pages and tabs within. After reading through their website, you should be able to summarize your findings, such as their location(s), products and/or services, competitors, history, etc. You can also visit the company's social media pages to find out the latest happenings. Reading everything on a company's website can seem overwhelming. To keep this step simple, pull out a piece of paper or a notepad. Notate everything that you feel is important to know about the company and position. Notating information will give you a better understanding of what you have read and it will make it easier for you to retain the information. Afterwards, you can always review your notes to refresh your mind with important content, rather than reading through multiple pages on the company's website.

In addition, you should know who will be interviewing you. Know their role in the organization. Search their profiles on LinkedIn to see if you can find a bond.

During the interview, if you are able to mention, "We have both graduated from the same college" or "I have also majored in Business Administration like you", it will demonstrate your interest in working for the organization and your time spent to prepare.

If you get the opportunity, talk to the employees or those who have recently interned there. Ask them about the culture or other information that can help you during the interview. The more you talk about the company and position, the more you learn. The more you know, the more impressive you can be.

Preparation

Thoroughly read and analyze the job description to figure out what is most important to the employer. This is the answer sheet to the interviewer's questions. It will tell you the background, skills, and qualifications they are seeking. For example, if you are interviewing for a cold calling sales position, the job description most likely states that the employer prefers you have previous cold calling experience. That may or may not be the deal breaker, but they also most likely want know if you're confident and persistent. Make sure you fully understand the job description. Sometimes employers do list abbreviations and industry terms that you may not be familiar with. If there is anything that you do not understand, make sure you research the meaning or reach out for assistance. If you meet their preferred qualifications, stress your skills and experience during the interview. Your resume is merely a short summary of your experience. The interview is your opportunity to tell them more about yourself.

Most importantly, make sure to sell yourself.

After you've reviewed the job description, ask a friend to set up a mock interview for you as practice. Give your friend a copy of your job description before you begin. It will help your friend prepare better suited questions. After the practice interview, ask for candid feedback to help you overcome any shortcomings. Practicing will not only better prepare you, but it will boost your confidence for the actual interview.

If you don't have anyone available to assist you with a practice interview, find a mirror. You can start off by saying "Hello" with a friendly smile. Being able to view yourself and your body language is exactly what the interviewer will be seeing. Do you see room for improvement?

If you or your friend needs sample interview questions, keep in mind that many interviewers still use basic questions such as:

"Tell me about yourself."

"Tell me about your position with your previous employer."

"Why are you interested in this position?"

"Where do you see yourself in the next five years?"

The best practice is to rehearse your response in advance. You can find many frequently asked interview questions in a later chapter to use for practice. Make sure your responses aren't too short, too long, or too generic. Give your answers your own personality. Don't worry if you feel you need further guidance in answering interview questions. We will discuss this further in a later chapter as well.

Questioning the Interviewer

Prepare several questions to ask the interviewer about the position, company, and day-to-day responsibilities. Write the questions down on a notepad enclosed in a business portfolio to bring with you to the interview. This will come in handy in case you don't remember the important questions you had in mind when the time is up. Having the questions written down shows you've dedicated time to prepare for the interview. Can you guess what that means to the interviewer?

If you want to get hired, asking questions is not optional, it is required. If you don't ask questions, don't expect to hear back from the interviewer. Asking questions shows the interviewer that you are truly interested in the position. There isn't a hiring manager out there that will hire someone that does not show interest in the position. Unfortunately, it's going to take more than showing up for the interview to prove that you're interested in the position.

Know the Route

Know the route to your interview location and figure out how long it will take you to get there with typical traffic. You cannot be late for an interview, regardless if it's for an entry level position or management role. Being late for an interview shows the interviewer that you have attendance issues. If you're not familiar with the area, take a trial drive to familiarize yourself with the route. Figure out where traffic usually builds up, additional routes in case of an accident or construction, where you are able to park, and how much time the commute usually takes. This is a simple step that can save you time and frustration if the unexpected ever comes up.

Prepare Business Attire and Interview Material

It is best to prepare your business attire and all of the material needed for the interview at least the day before. You don't want to be scrambling around last minute because you thought you knew where you last placed your tie, or if you thought your shirt was ironed. Your clothes should be clean and wrinkle-free. It is highly recommended that you put away at least two pens, a notepad, and several copies of your resume inside of a business portfolio. When scheduling the interview, you should always ask who you will be interviewed by and how many people you will meet with. By knowing how many people you will meet with, you will have a good idea of the amount of resume copies you should have printed. It's best to play it safe but printing out a few more copies than needed.

Prior to the interview, send an email to your references to give them a heads up, that way they are prepared to receive a phone call from the company you are interviewing for. During the interview, you may be asked for the contact information of your references, so make sure to have that ready. If you happen to be interviewing for a position such as a

Graphic Designer, Tattoo Artist, or Hair Stylist, bring examples of your work in a portfolio, as the interviewer will most likely want to take a look at your work.

Final Moments

On the day of the interview, put your phone on silent. You don't want your phone to be a distraction during the interview. You can leave it inside your car if you choose, but as long as it's silent, it shouldn't be a distraction. Typically, you want to arrive at least 15 minutes before the interview begins. This is what the interviewer will most likely recommend, if he or she even brings it up. While I agree that it's good advice, I wouldn't say it's great. I recommend you show up at least 30 minutes early. Why 30 minutes early? Think of the opportunities you can take advantage of with extra time. The extra 15 minutes of time before you check in can be used in many ways. It can save you in case of an accident, it can be useful if you're experiencing trouble with parking, or for anything unexpected. You can even use the extra time to practice interview questions to better prepare yourself. If you feel ready, you can use the time to arrive early to chat with an employee onsite or even observe the workplace. You may find a pamphlet with information, notice something interesting that you can bring up for small talk during the interview, or you may even be able to get some pointers from the receptionist. The receptionist or gatekeeper may share their impression with the hiring manager, so it's important that you keep a good impression.

Chapter 9: The Strategy That Is Communication

No matter how you look at it, communication forms an integral part of your life. It is unthinkable to exist without talking to each other. Interestingly, even without saying a word aloud, we will always be communicating. In the same way, job performance relies heavily on communication. Saying that communication is effective means that there is a shared meaning and understanding. There is no chance of getting hired after a job interview if you are endowed with poor communication skills. The question is how you can make sure that you stand out as a good communicator during an interview. Well, it starts with drawing the right communication strategy and working on it. Good communication is the conveyance of the right information and giving the right feedback through appropriate channels. It is the use of these channels that most interviewers will be looking for in a potential employee. Let's take a look at some of them.

Focusing on and rehearsing speaking skills

Any employer will be looking for someone who is practically perfect when it comes to words articulation but will hesitate to hire an applicant who is whispering out answers during an interview. You should make it clear that you are good speaker from the time you enter an interview room and exchange pleasantries with members of the interviewing panel. If you are unsure of how good your skills are when it comes to speaking, rehearse and have someone listen to you before walking into the interview room. Some people rehearse their speaking skills before a mirror, which is equally effective as long as you mean business.

Gaining composure

Using too many gestures to convey a message or respond to a question can be very irritating and even intimidating. In a job interview, this predicament would obviously be a bad one. Your chances of being hired will have plummeted to zero. A job interview is an official setting that requires professional but interactive communication. Make it easier to be understood by limiting your usage of gestures. Your facial expression during an interview should also show that you are composed and responsive. There is no way that you will be hired for a job after the interview if your facial expression is constantly a frown or indicates that you are not interested in the job. Develop a facial expression that is sure to create warmth in the interview room. It is also imperative that you rehearse proper posture before the interview, especially if you are not accustomed to it. Taking these into consideration will surely boost your chances of being hired.

Audibility and eye contact build confidence

If you have ever attended a job interview before, did you look down throughout the session? How often did you maintain eye contact with the interviewers? Confidence during an interview can be gauged based on many aspects, including you maintain eye contact with those asking you questions. However, the eye contact should not be so intense or extended as to come off as defiance. Keep it soft, but not to the extent that it will also portray you as shy person. If this is unimaginable, the best way to go about getting it right is through practice and rehearsal before you attend your next interview. Practice makes perfect, and rehearsing properly reflecting your confidence is a sure way to boost this undoubtedly important skill. For practice, you can have a few friends, and maybe a few strangers, ask you questions and try to respond while maintaining friendly eye contact. In fact, through proper eye contact, you can win the trust of a prospective employer and crush a job interview instantly.

Another aspect of confidence that will keep you on par with your competition during an interview session is audibility. How loud are you when responding to questions? Perhaps you have never been hired because whenever you attend a job interview, the way you respond to questions can be interpreted as shouting. However this is a curable problem. The best way solve the problem of shouting answers during a job interview is, as always, to practice, which will help you develop the right pitch and voice intonation.

Dress code as a first impression

You will similarly never be hired if you attend job interviews without paying proper attention to your dress code. An interview is not always only about being knowledgeable or having an outstanding resume supported by a dozen testimonials. How you dress is equally important and is sure to give you a competitive edge when it comes to scoring high and crushing a job interview. Dress code is a powerful non-verbal cue that interviewers will use to determine, among other things, your communication skills and attention to detail. Always be sure to confirm with your mirror, friend, or spouse that you are properly dressed for an interview before leaving the house.

Chapter 10: Preparing For Questions

There are three main categories of questions that will be asked during the interview: general, technical, and behavioral. As mentioned earlier, a good place to start researching the types of questions you should expect is on the web, particularly Glassdoor.com, or other question and answer sites, such as Quora.com or Yahoo Answers.

General Questions

While certain industries and positions will ask you different technical questions pertaining to those industries, every interview can be expected to have your basic questions. These questions are common, and the interviewer expects you will know these ahead of time (since they are easy to answer), but they are looking for how you respond to the questions. A simple internet search for interview questions will result in hundreds of useful results. I suggest you look through these and get a feel for general interview questions.

Technical Questions

Technical questions are really not something that any guide can prepare you for, because there are literally thousands of different industries out there and thousands of questions to accompany each industry. Technical questions are meant to test your knowledge on the terms specific to the industry your company operates in. It's assumed that you know the industry in which you are interviewing; otherwise you probably wouldn't have gotten the interview in the first place. However, talk to some people that work within the industry and ask them for some advice on what types of technical questions might be asked.

Behavioral Questions

Behavioral questions can be some of the most difficult. The interviewer's analyzing the answer to these questions more than any others. They will ask you a fairly open-ended question, based on a situation or experience, and then ask how you handled it. The **key** to answering these is understanding the reason *why* they are asking them. If you can understand why, then you'll be able to answer any of these questions with confidence. Later on we discuss the meaning behind certain types of questions, which will give you a good understanding of what to expect.

Not Knowing the Answer

Not knowing the answer to a question is not something that most people avoid, and in fact it is assured that you will almost always face one of these during an interview. After all, we can't know everything about everything, and that's okay. The interviewer doesn't expect you to know every answer to every question. What the interviewer wants to see, and what really matters, is how you respond. There will be times on the job when you don't know the answer to a particular problem. By being honest and upfront with your response, you are giving the interviewer what they want to hear. If the answer to the question baffles you completely, simply tell the interviewer that you don't know or you're not sure. If you somewhat know the answer, but aren't positive, explain what you know to the interviewer and tell them that you aren't sure about the rest. The WORST way to approach it would be trying to make something up. This leads to the interviewer making a negative assumption about your overall personality traits and how you handle something you are unsure about. This, of course, only applies to technical questions, where there is a definite answer. If you were asked what your greatest strengths are, the "I don't know" wouldn't suffice at all.

Chapter 11: After The Interview

Congratulations! You've made it through the interview. You most likely now want to get out of there as quickly as possible, but there's an important procedure to follow before you leave. After the interview is formally finished, ask them, "how did I go?" Most interviewers will answer honestly and this can immediately let you know what your chances of getting the position are, and this definitely will not make your chances any worse. They may even give some areas for future improvement, which is great, and doesn't necessarily mean that you won't get the job. If you haven't been told already, you can also take the opportunity to ask when you'll find out if you've been a successful applicant. If you do ask this, try to sound excited and optimistic, as if you're preempting that you will be successful.

As you're leaving, emphatically thank the interviewer for the opportunity (it's okay to go over the top here). Another trick I've found useful in the past is to provide a hand-written note again thanking them and stating that you're looking forward to hear from them soon. Leave this with the receptionist and ask for it to be given to the interviewer at the end of the day. This will show that you're willing to go the extra mile and keep you fresh in their minds when it comes time to make their decision.

The hard work is now all done! You can relish in the fact that you've put your best foot forward and given yourself the best possible chance of getting the position. Now all that's left is to allow the employer to come to their decision. If you haven't heard back after an appropriate duration of time, don't hesitate to send a follow up email. A few days after the designated call back date, or if no date was set, two weeks after the interview, is a good time to send an email. Be courteous and try not to sound too needy, again thanking them for the opportunity to apply for the position, before inquiring as to when you will be informed of the outcome.

If you somehow after this valiant effort are unsuccessful in getting hired, try to find out why. Email back the liaison or interviewer to find out ways you can improve for future interviews. If nothing else this whole process will have been an excellent learning experience, and you'll be able to apply it again twice as well and twice as confidently when entering your next interview situation.

I honestly believe, though, that if you follow this procedure step by step, do thorough research and maintain a positive, confident mental state throughout the interview, there will be no other applicant who can even come close to you. But most importantly, you have to believe this yourself.

Chapter 12: How To Make A Lasting Impression On The Interviewers

Here are some final tips to help you make a great impression on your interviewers.

Dress Sharply

Your dressing does create a strong impression on your interviewers. If you don't look sharp and instead, are shabbily dressed, chances are you'll put off your interviewers and reduce your chances of landing that job.

Thus, ensure you dress formally and look neat. Shower on the day of the interview and make sure your hair is clean, nails are trimmed, and that you smell nice (not too overwhelming). Also, pay attention to your shoes: wear smart, clean shoes.

Carry Important Documents

While your interviewers will have a copy of your resume and cover letter, make sure you take along some spare ones with important documents related to your academics, educational institutions you studied in, and documents related to your past work experiences. This helps you come off as a responsible and smart individual who prepares well for situation.

Greet the Interviewers Nicely and Warmly

Upon entering the interview room, greet all the interviewers warmly and nicely. Extend your hand to each one of them for a nice, formal handshake. Ensure your hands are clean and smell nice, and keep each handshake firm, brief and gentle.

Maintain Direct Eye Contact

Throughout the interview, maintain direct eye contact with each interviewer in succession so you can come off as a confident person.

Engage the Interviewers

If an interesting topic comes up, one you know interests you and your interviewers, build on it to engage them. This helps you create a good impression on your interviewers.

In addition, interviewers may ask you a few questions related to the current affairs of the country. Therefore, read the newspaper a few days prior to and on the interview day to ensure you have succinct answers to such questions.

Chapter 13: Soft Skills

Can you share a time you've had to give bad news to a group of people?
This is a question on your ability to communicate. If you've been a leader and you had to share that the compensation plan was changing or there would be an entire new way of doing business, that's the example they are looking for. Did you have a process when you had to communicate something challenging? How do you prepare? Do you anticipate comments and challenges others may have? Is it an emotional topic that may make it hard for you to share perspective?
No matter what your example is, remember all the questions above and roll it together to show you have a process (top of the funnel) and then give your example.
Winning answer:
These are the toughest types of communication. It's important that, no matter how I feel about it, I provide

context and help others to the point of supporting the overall direction of the company. I go through a mental checklist. I ask myself, how did I feel when I first heard the news? What's the positive and what will they perceive as negative? I try hard to anticipate comments and potential challenges, and I prepare a thoughtful statement. Then, if I have enough time, I practice the message, either with a peer or a trusted advisor. Here's an example of how I did this and the results of that meeting....

If you have no example of a challenging communication you had to share, it's all right. Talk through your process on ALL communication (similar to the questions above) and how you could share any communication that could have gone south, but because of your preparedness, you could keep it positive.

How Do You Handle Working with Difficult Co-Workers?

Interviewers ask this question to know about your interpersonal skills or how you relate to people. It's easy to relate to those who are easygoing, but you can really differentiate yourself by showing your strong interpersonal skills with those who may be perceived as difficult. The way you answer this question shows interviewers a glimpse of your character.

An additional part of this question may be implicit, specifically, how do you define "difficult" coworkers. Your answer can speak volumes about how you see most people at work.

The best answer usually falls under the category of looking for ways to productively and positively deal with the challenger. It shows the ability to be a level-headed diplomat and demonstrates you do not thrive on drama and emotion. Above all, you become a stronger asset to the firm.

Winning answer:

Generally, there are 3 ways to deal with challenging types: head on collisions, running away and hiding from such people, and looking for ways to y deal with them productively and positively. A challenging type might be one always negative and does their best to put negative thoughts in the greater team's minds. It can be a person who is just unhappy with their lot in life and wants others to join in their misery. It may also be a person who just "doesn't get" the vision of the firm. When someone is "challenging," I do my best to provide myself as an ally to them and a buffer to others. What I mean by that is I give the challenging person a sounding board and try to help them see different perspectives. I share the good they are doing, and I try to catch them doing the opposite of their norm, and I thank them for it publicly. Sometimes, it works.... Recently, I had this situation come up.... "-----" If this doesn't work and they are just too difficult to work with and integrate into our greater team, I separate myself, and I hold myself to the highest standard as an example. You can't change everyone, but everyone deserves a chance.

How Well Do You Adapt to Changes?

Many industries are in constant flux. Emphasize your natural skills, character traits, and your talents as the means by which you're able to adapt well and adapt fast. It's best to back it up with a short, but clear, example of a previous experience.

Winning answer:

Few industries are static and without change. I wouldn't say change is my favorite thing to experience. I like to have a process and work towards that process to see success. However, it's important to be adaptable. The times I've had to adapt and adjust or recreate my processes have been times when I've excelled. I work backwards from the end state, "best result" to see how to adjust my process. An example of this is when my small firm Fox Limited was purchased by Wolf Enterprises. We did not know what to expect. We didn't even know if we would have jobs after the acquisition. The best thing I could do was stay positive and work hard in the framework of what I knew it was to succeed. Over time, more became apparent on our current roles and how they would shift. I learned what the desired result was, and I focused on adjusting my existing winning process to include the nuances to win in a slightly different way. I was a top performer in the old firm, and I am a top performer in the new firm.

Chapter 14: Never Make Assumptions In The Interview

This is a good piece of advice to follow in life, but it also has a special place in an interview setting. You want to be viewed as someone who understands what is required and can deliver the expected results – more than just in the interview room – and making assumptions will not guarantee you will be viewed like this. The easiest and best way to avoid assumptions is to always ask for clarification. If a question is asked that is ambiguous or you really aren't sure what they mean, ask for explanation. Sometimes, without meaning to, an interviewer will use company jargon or acronyms in a question or in conversation. You can respond by saying, "I'm sorry, I'm not familiar with that term, could you explain it to me please?" Not only will this show that you are paying attention but it will also demonstrate that you have an interest in the company and what they are about.

When you are answering a question and you need to include company specific terminology, be sure to explain what you mean and keep it in basic terms. You should never assume that your interviewer will know what you are talking about. Take a moment to either set up your answer with the required information to understand what you are talking about or pause and explain the meaning of certain phrases or words. Better yet, it best to use common terms in the place of company specific ones.

Lastly, **NEVER** assume that the job is in the bag. No matter how confident you are that you are the most qualified person for the position – it isn't yours until you have received a job offer. Make the best impression you have and keep the mindset that you are still competing for the job and sell yourself accordingly.

Show Enthusiasm In The Interview

You are most likely excited at the prospect of getting a new job and thrilled that you were called in for an interview? Well, then show it when you are being interviewed!

Bring energy and a positive attitude to the interview that will make the company take notice. You should project this image in your demeanor, facial expressions, and most importantly in the content of your answers. The process of interviewing is usual a long and boring one for those on the other side of the table so do your part to make it easier for them to choose you as the best candidate. Just think there are a number of people being interviewed before and after you for the same position. You can try to setup apart from the rest by being enthusiastic and smiling when answering (when appropriate) and still maintain an aura of professionalism.

You want to convey charisma and keep the interviewer's attention. They have heard a lot of the answers already, but you can get the message across with more than words.

Someone who is excited to get a job and lets the excitement be known is going to have a better chance than someone who talks in a monotone and with little to no emotion. Don't be afraid to smile and use phrases as "that's great" or "wonderful" when you are told about the company. Be the type of person that the company wants to represent them and you will increase the chances of a job offer. Be genuine in your enthusiasm and just be yourself. If Sincerity is the focus of your enthusiasm it should work for you instead of against you. If you are naturally bubbly by nature, tone it down a bit for the interview so you do not overwhelm your hosts.

Explaining Gaps In Your Employment

Be prepared to discuss you resume when you get to the interview and to explain why you left previous companies as well as any gaps in employment. Many people are fearful that an interviewer is going to discover that they were without a job for a period of time. It is not necessarily a discouraging thing, but you do have to be able to tell the interviewer why in the best possible light. You should always be honest when explaining any absence from work during an extended period of time. For instance, if you were laid of your job and had a hard time finding a replacement but spent a lot of time with your children you could say, "I took an opportunity to spend a few months with my children in between jobs." If you took any courses or classes that adds value to your skills as an employee be sure to mention that as well.

You may find it beneficial to add a brief explanation on the resume itself or in a cover letter. Most times it is hard to get to an interview if there is a lengthy and unexplained employment gap.

If you are uncertain of what possible questions could be generated from your resume, have another person look at it. It is best to be prepared for unspecified questions and scenarios that will likely come up in an interview. You do not want to be caught stumbling or floundering for an answer. Give yourself time to figure out the best explanation for times of unemployment so an interviewer sees it as reasonable or even beneficial to them in the case of additional education and classes.

Adhere To Etiquette During The Interview

During an interview you need to be mindful of your manners and follow an unspoken code of etiquette. Business manners are going to be key, because an interview is so much more than what you have to say – it is how you present (or sell) yourself. If part of the job you are applying for is dealing with clients or executives from other companies, you can be guaranteed how you act and mannerism is part of the decision making process. You must be able to maintain eye contact without being uncomfortable. It's is okay to glance away when gathering your thoughts but if you are listening to someone keep your attention focused on them (even if their eyes are wandering). This shows good manners and that you care about what they have to say.

Having Gum or a mint in your mouth during the interview is totally unacceptable. If you want to be sure that you have fresh breath, chew gum or suck on the mint before arriving at your destination but discard or finish them before you enter the building. It is distracting and rude to have them in your mouth when answering questions. Always refer to the interviewer's by name, ideally you found out who you would be interviewed by when the meeting was arranged. When you arrive, shake hands and greet the person by name. If you are just learning their name, repeat it and remember it. You want to be sure to get it right and thank them for their time when you are leaving.

Make A Connection With The Interviewer(s)

If you are interviewing for a highly sought after job then you will have a lot of stiff competition. An outstanding interview is crucial to make you stand out from the rest of the crowd. To give yourself an added edge and cement yourself in your interviewer's mind, try to make a personal connection with them at some point in the interview. A personal connection can take numerous forms. If you are in the interviewer's office and they have a picture of a dog on their wall (and you happen to love dogs), make an appropriate comment that identifies you as a dog lover too. This may not put you above others more qualified than you but it will help you to stand out amongst those you are in direct competition with.

Take your cues from the interviewer, if they seem uncomfortable with relaying any personal information or are not comfortable veering off topic then follow their lead. If a personal conversation does develop, let the interviewer guide it. When they bring it to a close and either get back to the questions or say good bye, leave it at that. At the end of the day, interviewers want to hire people that are qualified and fit with the rest of the team at the company. If you can make a connection and have the right skill sets you will most likely have a better chance than someone else. You will also stick out in the interviewers mind as the candidate who knew a lot about dogs. If you are not comfortable with discussing personal topics during an interview, don't feel that you must go out of your way to do so. At the end of the day, your qualifications are what you should be highlighting.

Asking Questions After The Interview

When you make it to the end of your interview and the interviewer asks if you have any questions for them. There are some questions that you ask and some that you simply do not ask.

DO NOT ASK: "How did I do" and "Are you going to hire me"

ASK: "What are the next steps and the timeline for them to make a decision"

ASK: "What is the company's direction and expansion"

ASK: "Based on your research ask any company specific questions"

ASK: Asking about salary is acceptable if it has not already been outlined.

Look at the opportunity to ask your own questions as your chance to interview the company. Show your preparedness and pull out the list of prepared questions based on the research that you have done. Feel free to take notes; it can earn you brownie points. Ask questions that are important to you as well, if vacation time and benefits are a deal breaker for you, find out now what the company has to offer.

The Panel Interview

A one on one interview is stressful enough but it's even worse when two or more people are asking you questions and watching your every move. This situation may not intimidate everyone, but it is certainly not a comfortable position to be in. The rationale for a panel interview is to get the opinion of multiple people at the same time on the viability of a work candidate. In general the people that attend are from various departments within the company – a representative from human resources and the department that is hiring at a minimum. This lets the interviewers see how the candidates react under pressure.

When you are listening to questions during a panel interview, maintain eye contact with the person who is speaking. Once the question has been asked, make sure to address your answer to all who are present. Make eye contact with everyone and include them in your attention. Be prepared for follow-up questions from any or all of the attendees. Each one is going to want to know information from an angle that will directly affect their department. In some panel interviews, only one person does the talking and everyone else is there simply to observe. Never the less address all of your comments to the group and don't let this unnerve you. It is absolutely stressful, but not unusual. Be grateful that they consider you a strong enough candidate to gather more than one person to evaluate you as a potential employee for the company. An interview is an investment for a company, an expenditure of money in the form of salaries; you are there because you have a chance at the position so take advantage of the opportunity.

Chapter 15: Expectancy Of Employers And Their Tactics

An interactive interview is the best way to recognize if a candidate's appearances and behavioral traits are essential in your open business. In addition to this in a social meeting the questioner asks the candidate about an instance that happened in the past in a particular organization in which a particular behavior was showed and expected the candidate to identify a specific scenario that happened, the best way to answer this kind of question is for the candidate should not be aware of the conduct that the questioner is proving.

During a real interview, the interviewer needs to know the candidate's behavior trait and the type of job described. Sincere work makes the meeting operative and fruitful. For you to conduct an active communicative interview here are some of the tips that you need to follow:

Tips to Conduct an Effective Behavioral Interview

- You need to make a list of questions to ask every candidate when conducting the communicative interview; the questions must be both behavioral and traditional. The interactive interview queries give you the platform to compare the numerous answers and approaches that you got from other candidates. This makes the candidate selection more defendable.
- You need to find the list of the main behavioral personalities you have faith in that an applicant desires to be gifted to perform the work you are going to offer.
- Ask for the list of both communicative and outdated queries that you made of every candidate through the communicative interview.
- Plan interviews with the applicants who most seem to have the behavioral features, along with the aids, knowledge, schooling, and other aspects that you need, and you usually display for in your submission review.
- Narrow your candidate's choices based on the answers they give to the

communicative and outdated interview queries

- You also need to choose your applicant with the right mix of information, involvement, and communicative traits that goes hand in hand with the job guiding your decision.
- Inscribe a job position that pronounces the behavioral traits of the candidates you need in the text. Ensure that the characteristics of the qualification segment of your work explanation list the same communicative traits.
- Identify the features and traits of the person whom you have confidence will flourish in that job. If you have the workers who perform positively in the job presently, list down the qualities, features, and services that they bring to the work which makes the job successful.
- You also need to identify and list the mandatory yields and presentation success aspects for the work opened.
- Recognize what you need the worker to be able to do in the openwork that you are going to offer. A job description and job

specification are needed to define the necessities of the spot untaken.

- Note the applicants who have pleased you and caught your devotion with their credentials and experiences to supplementary shorten the list of the candidates needed in the interview. You want to plan the most competent applicants for a communicative interview.
- Assess the resumes, cover letters, and other work submission constituents you received from the candidates with the behavioral characters and features in awareness.

For a candidate to be employed by the employer in the open job advertised, the employer expects to see the following characteristics and traits when conducting a behavioral interview.

Characteristics and Traits Expected by The Employer During A Behavioral Interview

Articulate

When you are able to express your thoughts and feelings easily and clearly in that you can speak fluently and coherently without any fear during the behavioral interview. This enables the employer to know that you will be able to express your feelings without fear of getting embarrassed anytime you see something that should not be done in the organization and when it is something recommendable you will also be happy and motivated.

Accountable

You need to be responsible for whatever you do in the workplace, and you must give a satisfactory reason for doing it. The candidate should be able to report any incident to the employer or explain something that needs to be done in the organization.

Listener

The candidate should be a good listener in that he or she needs to listen carefully to the questions being asked carefully during the behavioral interview and the candidate needs to answer them correctly.

Perseverance

You should be able to persistently do something despite difficulty or delay in achieving success. You will be required to put continued effort without being tired to do or achieve something despite difficulties, failure, or opposition in a particular task once you are hired. This will make the employer know that you are persistence in any task given to be done. In other words, being self-minded.

High energy

This is when you are active and faster at all times at work, and anytime you are given the assignment to work on, you are able to complete it at the correct time and submit it because time is of the essence, and time management is effective.

Confident

The candidate should be confident while answering the questions that he or she has been asked by the employer. The confidence applied will enable the employer to identify your confidence skill, and you will be good to go.

High integrity

You need to be highly intelligent in that you should be in a position to answer any question you have been asked by the employer during the behavioral interview.

This will make the employer know that even when you are given a particular task to tackle when hired you will be in a position to do it perfectly.

Self-directed

This is the act of making your own decisions and organizing your own work rather than being told. It helps a lot because you can decide what is best and needed in the project or task you are told to do by the employer.

Adaptable

You are required to adapt faster and get used to the new way of operating and doing different tasks in the new place you are hired. To adapt faster will enable you to know how a lot of things are done within a short period of time.

Focused

The candidate should show that he or she is focused on the type of job going to be offered to him. In other words, the candidate should show hard-working skills because it is one of the skills that the employer notices first. If you are focused it will give you a high chance of being employed.

Money hungry

This is when you really want money, trying to get money or strongly desiring money. The act of strongly desiring money in that you are actively doing your job and in a perfect way that the employer remains to admire.

Enthusiastic

You should be able to show intense enjoyment, interest, or approval in a project given to you by the employer once you are hired. This will show the employer that you are enjoying your job and that you are showing interest in it.

Chapter 16: After The Interview

You answered questions and you asked questions. The interview is over. You got a company business card and, hopefully, you have a business card from your interviewer. You now can start working on the follow up stage. This could be a determining factor of whether you get the job or not. This is a step that many people overlook. Sometimes, they feel that the interview went so well or so bad that they don't follow up. You can go from being an exceptional candidate to just an okay candidate from the lack of follow up. Someone who was an okay candidate can go to being an exceptional candidate because they took the initiative to go a step further with the interview process.

It is very tempting to be creative after the interview to grab the attention of the interviewer, but it is not appropriate to send a gift as a thank you to anyone working at the company you wish to join as the next new hire. Do not send flowers, candy, or anything that may have come up in conversation during the interview. Your act of kindness could be viewed as an act of bribery.

Do not attempt to directly connect with any employee from the company on social media. Do not request to contact the interviewer on LinkedIn, Instagram, Facebook, Twitter, or any other form of social media. It's one thing to view their pages and sites for the job interview research but it's another thing to attempt to connect and bond with employees on social media. This is not going to be impressive and could hurt your chances of getting hired.

Prepare the thank you correspondence right after the interview. Don't wait to follow up on your interview. If you were not able to get an email address, type a thank you letter to be mailed the next day if you can't get it out by mail the day of the interview. If you received an email address, send a thank you email within 12 hours of the interview.

The thank you correspondence is meant to reinforce how you will be a good fit for the company and how you took the interview seriously as a candidate. This is your last chance proving that they should hire you.

How do you write a thank you letter? The thank you letter should be tailored directly to the person or persons that interviewed you. If you interviewed with more than one person, email everyone that interviewed you individually, and do not send one email addressed to a group of employees. If you are mailing a letter, send everyone an individual letter.

Example:

Dear (Name),

Thank you for meeting with me today regarding the (job title) opportunity. I thoroughly enjoyed learning more about the team and position, and I'm very excited about the opportunity to join (company name) and help with bringing (value your position offers such as sales, exceptional management skills, etc.) to your team/department.

I look forward to hearing from you about the next steps in the hiring process. Do not hesitate to contact me if you need further information from me. Thank you again for the opportunity and for your time.

Sincerely,

(Your name)

Now that we have covered what needs to be done before and after your interview, good luck. You are prepared to get hired.

Chapter 17: Post Interview - Saying "Thank You"

Post-interview, within the week, you will want to send a professional "thank you" letter to your interviewer(s) to show your gratitude for being invited to interview for a potential position. Be sure to indicate your gratefulness. This also reiterates the fact that you are still interested in the job and reminds them of your positive attitude and of your strong qualities, which you would have displayed or mentioned at the interview.

A handwritten "thank you" note is always a good way to express your gratitude to the interviewer for their time and consideration during the interview. It serves as a great personal touch and is recommended for post-interview.

In addition to the "thank you" note or letter, you can also call the office and politely make them aware that you are excited about the prospect of working with them in the future. Let them know you are still interested and tell them that you are open to hearing about the hiring choice from the interview.

Final Thoughts

Plan, prepare, execute and hope for the best. If it does not work out with a particular job the first time, have a strategy you plan to follow to eventually get the job you want. The last thing you want to do is get discouraged. Not every interview will work out, but if you follow the steps in this book closely, you will increase your chances of getting called back. Do not forget to use your network. Let your friends and family know what your next career move is so that they can be an extension of your ears to listen for new opportunities that suit your vision.

Remember, first impressions are the most important because they cannot be recreated. Be yourself and be a good listener. You will want to recollect information relayed by the interviewer should you be offered the job.

All the best in your endeavors. We hope this guide has been helpful and insightful in your search for the best job suited for you.

Chapter 18: Preparing For The Informational Interview

Preparing for the Interview

As you prepare for the informational interview, there are a few things to keep in mind to ensure maximum success. Here is the situation: The interviewee has presented you with an extraordinary opportunity in that he or she thought highly enough of you to grant you an interview. If you go into the interview and simply begin asking questions that reflect a lack of preparation and organization, you will appear unprofessional, and chances are the interviewee will not take you seriously. I cannot underscore enough the importance of being prepared before you go into the interview.

Being prepared means the following:

You have double-checked your questions to ensure they align with and are specific to the interviewee, the job, the organization, or the industry.

You have written down your questions and prioritized them so that the most important ones get answered before your interview time expires.

You have developed and reviewed your resume to ensure it is tailored to meet the requirements of the job(s) you are interested in applying to within the interviewee's organization.

If you are meeting face-to-face, be sure you dress as appropriately. Because this is an informational interview, there is no need for business attire. Business casual would be appropriate for this type of interview. Just remember, business attire is absolutely warranted for a **job interview**.

You have mapped out the meeting location and accounted for travel time, tolls, etc.

You know something about the organization, meaning you have familiarized yourself with the website. Remember, you do not want to ask questions you can easily find on the company's website.

If meeting by phone, you ensure that you have a quiet place to chat, free of any distractions.

If traveling to the interviewee's location to meet, you have their phone number and email handy in case you have to contact them prior. For example, you can call the interviewee to inform them if you are running late.

Chapter 19: The #1 Techniques To Enhance Your Success

1. Persistence is Key
You cannot expect to achieve success overnight in business. You may ask a person to vouch for you that you know that works in the company. This is not to say that you will use the connection to move right to being hired, but at least it will let the company know that you would be a good addition to their organization.

2. The process of the interview is two-way
Yes, it is normal to let the recruiter lead the process, but you should also prepare to interview him/her. This is perfectly natural after all you are going to be in the company if you are accepted so the hiring manager will not be offended. Just picture the interview with just them asking you questions, and you putting or adding nothing to the conversation other than answering their questions. It may seem

like you are just trying to get the interview over with as soon as possible.

3. Be part of the company even when you are still in the application process

Before you have your interview make a list of things that you can do, beside each item mark those that are needed by this particular company. Read them and memorize them. If there is other requirement that you cannot at this point provide them with, start learning them and finding out more about them.

When the recruiter asks you "what can you contribute to the company?" You will know your answers because you took the time to memorize them. If the topic goes towards the things that you are not trained in yet you will at least have a basic knowledge about them. This will show the recruiter that you are eager to learn about them and expand your knowledge.

4. References Make a Big Difference

When you are submitting a resume make sure that you have the proper people listed as your references. You should gauge your references according to the position that you are applying for. Make sure that you warn people ahead of time that you have used their name as a reference. Make sure that the people that you choose are in good terms with you.

5. You need to practice, practice!

There is nothing wrong with practicing for your interview. You can easily do this alone by facing a mirror and rehearse the answers that you are planning on giving your interviewer. Watch to make sure that you are using proper posture and are speaking clearly. Ask a friend or family member to pretend to be the recruiting manager and let them lead the interview.

Chapter 20: Masquerade – The Phone Interview

I have never been a fan of the phone interview. It doesn't matter which side of the conversation I'm on, I don't feel like I can get a sufficient idea of the person on the other end.

Seeing beyond the mask of the phone

When you are offered the dreaded phone interview, let the company know you would be more than happy to schedule a face-to-face meeting with the interviewer and give them your schedule. Sometimes, the situation is set up specifically to interview over the phone. In those cases, you have to win the interview by using only your voice. You have no physical interaction, no body language, no eye contact--all you can use is the inflection of your voice to get your points across, disallowing some of the advantages that could help you stand out otherwise. Beyond that, you also have to deal with the unpredictable (and inevitable) services of the phone companies: dropped calls, bad or no reception, static, and volume difficulties.

I was interviewed over the phone for one position, even though I insisted I wouldn't mind coming in for an in-person interview. The company had an interview system where the applicant was first given a screening interview over the phone, then advanced to a phone interview with the Vice President of the company, and once the group of applicants was narrowed, they would begin calling people to come in for a third interview. It wasn't my favorite scenario, but it was the hand I was dealt in this situation. I still did my homework in researching the company and prepared my questions for the interviewer. I even cleared space in my day to be sure I didn't miss the phone call. As fate would have it, I'm a fairly practical person and the upgrading of my cellular device from my trusty flip-phone was unnecessary, though that often came with the dreaded dropped calls and horrible reception, so I wanted to be sure that I was in a full-bar area that was quiet enough for me to hear the interview questions and answer cleverly.

Being prepared as best I could for the uncontrollable variables, I picked up the call for the screening interview. It was a fairly short and pleasant conversation; though I'm sure I had to ask the interviewer to repeat the questions a couple of times. I felt that I had to overcompensate with my vocal inflection and witty comments since I could not show my interest in any other way. I had to make sure the conversation was comfortable enough that the screening would successfully push me forward to the next interview. Done.

For the second interview, my phone decided that it wanted to take a day off. I could not find a place that would give me full reception (come to find out, the cell phone towers in my area were down that day). The call dropped twice and I had to wait for a call back from the Vice President as he was calling from a blocked number, apologizing each time we reconnected. It made for a choppy conversation to say the least. I tried to jump on any piece of information that the VP gave to me to engage in the conversation and make it pleasant, but was unable to get a word in half the time. It becomes a war trying to battle for talking space. I was called for the third interview, but I felt it was by the grace of God--not from the phone interview.

The best thing one can do when asked to do a phone interview is to practice your vocal inflection more than anything else. If it helps, sit in front of the mirror while interviewing over the phone. Your facial expressions will aide your vocal inflection. Fluctuate your tone so as not to sound monotone and boring. Without any tools, other than speaking and listening, it can be hard to portray emotions genuinely.

As I mentioned before, I felt I was overcompensating with my voice to stand out from the other applicants. To me, this didn't seem genuine and the whole point of an interview is to get an honest understanding of the candidate. I also felt that I did not get a real feel for the interviewer. It is so important to have a perception of your potential supervisors and co-workers. With a phone interview, you aren't able to assess the environment that you would be working in with this potential position. How could you know if the environment, people and position are best for you and your personality?

Chapter 21: The Importance Of Research

Of course, you're too smart to blunder as flamboyantly as some misguided souls or behave like the job-hunter who took the interviewer's business card then proceeded to crumple it up and throw it in the wastebasket, in front of her. But if you're not prepared, it's still easy to be stunned into silence or begin babbling on about your life story—especially if you haven't anticipated certain questions.

Here's how you can research the job, a specific employer, and even the particular industry to avoid the number-one mistake job-hunters make: lack of research before the interview.

Researching the Job

Researching the job helps you measure your qualifications against what the employer wants, helps you think about examples you can give to prove you're the right person for the job, and tells you how the job may be different at this employer from others in the same industry. You also gain confidence and power in salary negotiation if you know you meet every qualification and then some. The more well informed you are, the better you come across in an interview and the greater your chances of landing the job.

Try to find the answers to these questions:
- What are the tasks and responsibilities?
- What are the qualifications for people hired for this job?
- What is a typical career path for a job like this?
- What are typical salaries?

This is where networking can be very helpful, whether it's a friend, colleague, friend of a friend, or information or a contact from a trade association or industry event. Read as much as possible in business and trade publications about the industry and employer to keep on top of career paths, hiring practices, and salaries (the last was often a closely guarded secret; no longer, thanks to the Internet).

Researching the Employer

Researching the employer never fails to impress the interviewer, since it shows you're serious and interested enough to do your homework. It immediately sets you apart from much of your competition, who are clueless as to the unique features of this specific employer.

Try to get answers to the following:
- What does the employer do?
- Who are its major competitors?
- How is it organized?
- What are its strong points?
- What are its weak points?
- What is the employer culture like?

An employer's website usually offers tons of useful information, from descriptions of different divisions, products and services, and future plans to financial information. Brochures and annual reports published by employers are invaluable sources as well. Some employers publish recruitment brochures, which describe training programs, employment policies, and other information job-hunters seek. Contact the employer's public relations department and ask for these materials.

Researching the Industry

Trade associations are very helpful sources of information on the industries they represent. Most publish newsletters that run articles on industry trends and news of interest to the industry. Many have extensive websites, as well as job referral banks.

Trade associations often host national conferences in addition to meetings and seminars held by local chapters, which often can be attended by nonmembers at a higher fee and which are goldmines of networking contacts as well as industry information. All have membership directories to encourage networking among members.

It's good to keep track of your job interviews in an orderly fashion, both to write down information acquired before the interview—from place, time, contact information, and research you've done—and after the interview, like follow-up required or more interviews with the same employer. Try to keep it in a folder or notebook. You'll go mad if you just do it on little scraps of paper.

Multiple interviews are common today, so don't be surprised if you're asked to come in five different times to meet with different people. That makes keeping track of each even more important.

Now you know two vitally important points that will immediately improve your job interviews: how to be prepared and how to put yourself in the interviewer's shoes. You've learned to be prepared by researching the job, employer, and industry so you're ready to answer questions and ask some of your own. You've also learned how to put yourself in the interviewer's shoes by understanding what they fear and what they hate. And last but not least, you know how to obtain and organize all this information before and after the interviews. You'll soon be acing them with flying colors.

A short thank-you letter should be sent after each interview, ideally the old-fashioned paper kind. You can personalize each with information in your notes. For example, perhaps one interviewer emphasized a specific aspect of the job, another attended the same college you did, and so on.

Chapter 22: Researching The Company

Look for information on the company online. This is a really good way of standing out as a candidate and if you are asked if you know anything about the company, you will be prepared to answer the question.

Type the company's name on a search engine such as Google or Bing to look for a web site. If you can find the company's web site on a search engine, click on it. Read the company's home page. If they have a page such as "About Us," read it. You want to make sure you read the company's Mission Statement. If they have information on press releases or company news, read as much as you can and don't be afraid to congratulate them on the positive news at the job interview. If company officers, managers, or other employees are listed, write down their names and titles. Knowing the name of the top boss is always impressive and shows that you did your research on the company. If the company lists some of their clients, this will give you an idea of the types of companies that does business with your future employer. Make sure you write a brief summary of the web site information on a notepad that you will take to the interview.

If the company doesn't have a web site, check for a Facebook or Twitter page. Log into Facebook or Twitter and search for the company's name. Look for their likes and comments. Follow the company. Don't restrict your social media search to only the company. You might also find employees listed. I just refrain from trying to friend an employee on Facebook until after you have the job offer.

A big source of information that can be found about companies is on the web site Glassdoor. Glassdoor provides information such as who is the owner or CEO of a company, what workers like and dislike about the company, what employees view as a need for improvement, salaries, benefits, and the interview process. This is very valuable information you can receive before you even speak to an employee at the interview.

If you cannot find a lot of information on the company from a search engine or if you are seeking to find employees, log into the web site LinkedIn. You can search for the company on the search bar under "Companies." Follow the company. If you know the name of the person you will interview with or if you know the name of the Human Resources personnel you spoke with over the phone, search for the person under "People" on the search bar. If you are able to find the person, go to their LinkedIn profile to find out information about them. Look to the side of the screen to see if anyone under the "People Also Viewed" show additional employees. If you find other employees, click on their name and view their profile. Check to see if you are connected to them and how you are connected. When it comes to who knows who, you could be amazed at how you are connected to someone who knows someone. Remember, do not attempt to request to be added as a connection. You are viewing for research of the company and not to come off as someone who knows no boundaries.

Chapter 23: Employee Hygiene And Welfare

In most of the organizations, very poor attention is being given to above topic. Especially in organizations governed under industrial employment law, special attention to be paid to hygiene and welfare. When the requirements are fulfilled it will be a satisfactory factor of auto building up of Employer / Employee sound / healthy relationship, which is of immense value to a company management. You have to determine that when employees are happy with work and environmental backgrounds, such organizations produce best results and best profits. We all must take immediate step whatever possible to create the situation. These are the general conditions that employers' should fulfill in an industrial environment.

Over crowding employees in an organization should be restricted. General universal standard is 400 cubic feet per person in a space, where height is less than 14 feet.

Reasonable temperature should be maintained in each work room so that workers could work in comfort. Suitable steps should be taken to maintain circulation fresh air in each work room and facilities should be provided to remove all fumes, dust and other impurities.

Sufficient and suitable lighting should be provided in every part of the factory in which persons are regularly working. For operations that need sustained attention, higher illumination should be provided. Lighting should be provided in such a manner as to avoid glare.

Sufficient number of sanitary conveniences with accessible water taps should be provided and maintained for male and female workers separately on the ratio of one per every 25 workers. Where number of male workers exceeds 100, urinals should be provided on the basis of one per every 50 males.

Washing facilities to be provided separately to males and females on the basis of one wash basin for every 20 persons employed at a time. Sufficient number of showers also to be provided wherever the workers need to take a shower bath after work.

A spacious meal room to be provided to accommodate workers to have their meals comfortably; drinking water, wash basins, soap & heaters also to be provided to meet requirements. If the meal room is not so spacious, attention to be paid to arrange group by group to occupy meal room.

There should be rest room employees to rest whenever they are not well. This is only to take a short rest when they experience a headache is a better arrangement if you can introduce a first aid box in the meal room.

Employees should pay special attention to introduce indoor games for during lunch break or any other free time.

Facilitating employees with visual and printed media to be considered for their leisure time

Industrial / labor relations

Industrial and labor relations of an organization are very important to the management and employees. There should be laid down principles with the concern of country's government labor authorities. In case if you follow Industrial / labor relations in an organization, you can minimize employee issues, unhappiness and other obstacles that will disturb to a smooth management. There are some measures to be adopted in this regard. Any person in need of information and important tips to pass an interview should definitely understand about so called measures and practice them. I give some tips about what should be implemented in establishing Industrial / labor relation standards in an organization. Shall we discuss about what should be implemented to maintain genuine Industrial / Labor relations.

The agreements between employer and employees with the involvement of labor department of the particular country - this

agreement to be subjected for study of employee representatives, management and the government body. After a thorough study it has to be signed by three parties, employer, representatives for employees and the authorized government body. Following aspects can be included in.
- Policy of paying salary
- Conditions of employment
- Disciplinary policy
- Policy of paying compensation
- Policy of gratuity payment
- Quality of product
- Policy of incentive payments
- Policy of retiring benefits

In the same manner you can include whatever policies you think that is important to the collective agreement. Once after three parties signed the collective agreement, no party is supposed to breach terms in the agreement. It will be very strong because the government has also one participant in the agreement. Both employer and employees will be very happy in performing their duties.

Employee councils

This is the latest concept that had been introduced to global employment sectors today. You can experience a new trend without the presence of trade unions. In modern world we have latest technologies, concepts to be introduced to employment sectors. Members will be appointed to employee councils from all sections, different personalities and to the management. Every decision will be a collective decision of the council whether it is in favor of employees or management. Nobody can oppose because every employment category is being represented. Decision of the council will be treated as final decision. There is no authority to over rule the decisions of employee councils. It is found that this is a very satisfactory concept because day to day problems in organizations are minimized and new concept helps smooth managing of establishments.

Internal communications

This is very important in managing organization. When we have a good internal communication system, every employee will be aware about company communications. Common practice is just informing by a circular to Head of departments and he is responsible in informing his / her staff about the contents of the circular. There are so many ways of communicating with employees and staff. Normally it's a practice to send memorandums, bulletins, and circulars as communication measures. We can sometimes see employers display big notice boards in Head office. In my opinion this is not a very successful method. Employee working at the interior end or in a branch, out side the premises will definitely not get this communication.

Emailing to all concern and displaying a printed matter in common places can produce better results. The communication should bet transparent to all members, it should reach up to bottom grass levels. It will be effective displaying the circular in canteen, meal room, paper reading arena and sports club etc.

Disciplinary procedure

It is a must that every establishment has their own disciplinary code. It is important to educate interviewees about company disciplinary procedures. New people joining companies will be really interested to know about company discipline and rules / regulations. Also it's good if we can enlighten new employees (who participate in job interviews) about disciplinary measures. Then they at least keep up to their discipline. It's a basic requirement to maintain discipline in a company. When the discipline is well maintained naturally the company will be well organized. In a disciplinary code following areas should be very well expressed.

- Attendance and punctuality
- Leaving office
- Absence with prior approval
- Absenteeism
- Verbal & written warnings
- Misconducts
- Work dress code
- Confidentiality of company information

- Conduct

Hours of work to be performed under different circumstances

Due to various work requirements in company's employees have to work under different circumstances. When the work is accumulated or when there are backlogs to clear some organizations introduce shift systems to enable to complete backlogs and turn the work process back to normal. In some reputed industrial organizations they introduce shift system permanently with intention of enhancing productivity.

On a normal working day – one shift operation

Monday to Friday 8 hours per day inclusive of an interval of half an hour for a meal or rest. Saturday a short working day of five and half hours inclusive of an interval for meals.

Two three shifts operation – Monday to Friday

Eight hours per day inclusive of an interval of half an hour for meals or rest. Saturday a short working day of five and half hours inclusive of an interval of half an hour for meals. For office employees, Saturday is a half day of five hours duration.

Night Work

There are no restrictions on employment of male workers on night shift. Employment of female workers on night work from 10 P.M. to 6 A.M, on the following day, will be allowed as a third shift subject to following conditions.

Written consent of the employee should be available. The employer to obtain prior approval from Labor department or government authorized body.

Payment of one and half times the daily rate of wages for the normal night shift. Maximum of 10 days night work per female worker in any one month.

A worker employed between 6 A.M. and 6 P.M. not be employed in night shift on same day.

An employee after night work to be allowed an adequate period for rest after such work.

Matron / female supervisor to be present during night shift.

Refreshments, medical and rest room facilities to be made available.

Transport facilities to be made available for use in an emergency.

Persons under the age of 18 years cannot be employed on night shift.

Grievance handling and Counseling

Special attention to be paid to Grievance handling and counseling as this is an important area which is neglected in some organizations. Employees perform work under an agreed employment contract but they may have some sort of grievance. Normally a worker never comes out with his / her grievance, supervisors, administrators and employers should no to identify their grievances. A good steady worker may decrease the speed and degree of work, this the point on which we should concentrate. It is our responsibility to speak to the particular worker and ask him whether we could help / assist him to get rid of the grievance. At this stage we should everything possible to put him right because workers are the best spirit of an organization. With your help & guidance you will observe that he comes to his normal spirit of working. It's very unfortunate in some organizations employers, senior managers and supervisory categories take no notice of such things. How can you expect a productivity enhancement or work development under circumstances.

As well when it is necessary we have to counsel certain employees. You have to be very vigilant and observant when identifying persons for counseling. Person may be working kith to kin but requirements are not fulfilled, his energy is being wasted. Such characters should be taken for counseling.

Important employee records to be maintained in a work place

This is a sole responsibility of the Human Resources department. A format should be available to issue to new people join to organizations. A personal file should be opened for every employer on the very first day. Copy of the person's letter of appointment, duly acknowledged by him should be filed in personal file. Copies of all other correspondence exchanged with employer should be filed accordingly. Warning letters, job description, salary increments, upgrading, promotions and work instructions issued to the employee should be recorded and filed methodically. Human Resources department is responsible to maintain personal information of employer. What personal information should be obtained from the employee?

Name and permanent address of employee

Contact telephone numbers

Temporary address, in case if the employee is boarded somewhere

Contact numbers of the boarding

Next of kin

Name of spouse

Information of dependents

Copy of employees National Identity card

Copy of passport or driving license

Copies of academic certificates

Copies of professional certificates

Copy of Birth Certificate

Employment categories

Also you should have a sound knowledge of employment categories as you are in a competition of passing job interviews. Persons attending job interviews should be thorough with employment categories. Under various administrative and management requirements employers prefer to appoint people for job vacancies on various categories.

Permanent Employment: Appointment letter expresses that you are appointed on permanent basis. Probably you will have to undergo a probation period (6 or 12 months) min accordance with the employment agreement. You will be eligible to enjoy all facilities and benefits of a permanent employee.

Fixed Term Contract Employment: This employment cannot be considered as a permanent employment. In your letter of appointment they clearly express that the employment is valued only to a certain period. (Probably for 6 months or 12 months) you will enjoy only certain facilities and some benefits under contract employment.

Casual employment: Casual employments are offered when companies have backlogs of miscellaneous work. Those employees have no rights to demand for work if they are asked to stay back when the entrusted work is completed. They are not regular workers in the company. Mostly they are being paid with daily wages or weekly wages as agreed upon. Employing casual persons is a risk because they will demand for continues work, whenever they are stopped unless otherwise they have been recruited on agreed terms with proper documentation.

Trainees / Apprentice

This category of employees is given opportunities to get themselves trained for work. Trainees/ apprenticed persons will be paid only a training allowance. They have to show excellent performances during training period, companies reserve all rights to stop them within training or after training if they are not found suitable to continue in employment. Trainees whose work evaluations are of a satisfactory standard will be confirmed after completion of training as permanent employees, on a probation period again.

Unskilled employees

Trainees come under this category, which need to be trained. Once after successful completion of

Training period, they become semi skilled employees. They are still to be trained to meet company requirements and to develop their job knowledge.

Semi skilled employees

Now you know who semi skilled workers are. They keep on applying for jobs with the intention of succeeding a permanent post elsewhere. That's the drive and initiative. They are keen to face interviews and get into some employment in order to gain experience. I have experience that there are some bright persons among them. If they can pass the interview with good merits, we should never hesitate to recruit them.

Now we have discussed everything relevant to the project and you should have brushed up your rust to pass interviews. When you want to pass an interview, you must plan your process very methodically. It is very rare they interview you to those traditional ways. Employers always prefer to recruit people who can win challenges, achieve goals and who can be flexible and adjustable under various situations. So first get through preliminary interview. Then concern about next interview, do the rehearsals we have taught you; you are sure to pass that interview. Then only the final hurdle will be there. Determine to pass, think positive, practice those interview exercises what we have introduced; get your intimates to help you doing interview rehearsals. Remember those top notches, interview techniques etc. You will certainly pass final interview. Do everything very methodically, the way I have given in examples.

We have guided you to achieve the above expected requirements and conditions. If you want to get through interviews, you have to be on your heels. Do not forget in an interview you compete with some other candidates, there itself you face a challenge. People who are serious to practice our tests introduced in this project can definitely pass interviews.

We like to see that you walk out from interview room with very positive and happy mind and determination. Even the interview board will be impressed upon you by observing your drive, personality and ambitious face.

Chapter 24: Optimize Your Resume

Before the hiring manager at the job of your dreams even sees you, he or she will most likely see your resume. Think of this one important document as the paper version of yourself. Just like you want to give a good first impression when you meet someone new, you want your resume to be able to make that first impression for you when you can"t be there yourself.

What Information You Must Include

Before you get to the creative part of optimizing your resume, you must gather some basic information that you will need to set it up. In addition to your name, address, telephone number, and email, here's some of the important information you need to have handy when you"re building your resume.

Education History

Ensure that important details such as email address, telephone number, and residential address provided in the resume are all kept up-to-date. The last thing you want while applying for a new job is to give out the impression of being a person who can't even take care to give out his personal details accurately.

Double check — if necessary, check for a third time — to make sure that you have spelt your name correctly in the document. Also, share the email address of an account that comes across as highly professional. This is something extremely important yet often undervalued. Think of it — if you were to choose between two individuals with email addresses as **andyprincecharming2000@gmail.com** and **andy.princep@gmail.com**, which one would you regard as more professional?

If you also have a website such as a portfolio page that highlights your past achievements and adds some more value to your job application, then don't forget to add it in the list as well.

Personal Statement

The personal statement section is one last chance you get on paper to really go out and market yourself. The three or four lines that you mention over here should really draw the attention of your potential employer and make them want to know more about the person you are and what you do.

A powerful personal statement can be created with the help of the following tips:

Keep things as simple as possible.

Maintain a consistent voice, whether first person or third person, and also ensure that you do not deviate from this anywhere in the resume. Do not begin with an "I am" and use "He is" a couple of lines down the order.

Tailor every personal statement as per the desired profile mentioned in the job description. An individual with proficiency in Microsoft Excel will surely be an asset for a desk job in an office but it may not serve any kind of purpose if you are applying as a yoga instructor.

Even if you have sought assistance from others in writing your resume, this is one section of the document that should be your own work. Also, read the file out loud to make sure that every bit of it reads well.

Avoid clichéd statements that bring in more confusion that clarification into the document. Phrases such as "From a very young age…" or "I have a thirst for knowledge"" don't really add up to anything.

With no more than 200 carefully chosen words, explain to your potential employer who you are, about your education, the skills and expertise that you have gathered, and the career goals you have set for yourself.

If you are looking for an appropriate example of what a good personal statement should look like, here is an example:

"I am a highly organized Business Management graduate and excellent communicator with two years' experience in the marketing industry. Looking to build upon the specific marketing and valuable transferable skills I have developed, I hope to continue to pursue a career in this fast-paced sector."

Training Courses and Other Professional Qualifications

This is the section where you should include all relevant training and education that you have gone through until that specific point in your career. The extent of details to be provided here will vary considerably depending on the level of education that you have attained, as well as the relevance that each level of education has to the desired job role.

If you just recently graduated, start by giving a complete description of your degree while also detailing the skills that you developed along the way. Remember that you should mention only the skills that hold some level of relevance and significance to the job. Your A-level results should follow this section in the form of a brief list.

All education information should be listed out in reverse chronological order, meaning that the qualification you have achieved the most recent should be listed at the top of the order.

Work Experience

If you happen to have many years of work experience behind you then including your voluntary work, vacation jobs, part-time jobs, and unpaid work experience won't provide any additional value to your resume. If indeed you want to include your charity work then the "Interests" section would be a better bet.

However, in the event that you have been through a period of unemployment, including these jobs can prove useful. The same applies for any duration in your career during which you were not working, whatever the reason! Also if you happen to feel that a part of the experience earned in carrying out these part-time jobs will be useful for your new job then don't forget to miss out on including it.

Remember to give some extra degree of concentration to the two jobs that you have completed in recent years because these are the details employers always show maximum interest in.

Have your most recent job, or the last place that you worked, listed at the top and then do a tracking back. For every position that you held, mention your job title as well as the job title of the person who was your immediate superior. Don't forget to mention the dates on which you started and ended in each of these positions. If ever you enjoyed an internal promotion in a project, mention that as well as an individual job role.

Don't forget to mention the name of the organization. In addition, include a brief description of the company, such as its industry and the services it aims to provide. Use the same terms that they use for describing themselves — the company website is a good place to start on your research.

You should also add the main skills, duties, achievements, and responsibilities that will prove useful when you join your new employer. Remember, they are looking for the candidate who will best suit their needs. Just as you are thinking "what's in it for me?"" when you look for a job, your potential new employer is also thinking the same thing when examining a list of job applicants.

Be specific while listing your skill-set and remain optimistic about being a good performer with these skills. Just saying "good communication skills" may not be enough but if you refer to it as "good written and oral communication skills" it gives your potential employer more insight into what kind of communication skills you are actually good at.

Don't forget to list the amount of responsibility you have held in every position. List the achievements that you have managed while in every position along the way along with improvements in productivity and cost savings that you may have helped in making. Quantify these achievements as far as possible. You should place at least some achievements in this section that can be relevant to the new job you are applying for.

Achievements

You should take care not to list more than four or five of the major achievements you managed at work. Any other achievement should be listed where you detail your work experience. Do not go about listing any and every achievement; mention only the ones that will be of relevance to your next job and also indicate how you went about achieving them.

This is one of the more important sections since you will only be called in for an interview if the employer thinks you are worthy of it and will bring some kind of benefit to the organization. Your achievements serve as an important tool to help market you thus putting you in a better place for earning employment than someone else. This is why you should give some serious consideration to your achievements.

Skills, Interests, and Hobbies

In this section, list out the interests and hobbies that could be of relevance to the new position you wish to take up as part of your new job role. **Relevance** is the key word here, as this is one area where people tend to go overboard. Stick to listing only those interests and hobbies that reflect your personality rather than filling in the lines with a whole lot of rubbish information that won't be of any value to anyone.

Thinking out-of-the-box can prove to be a major asset here because you never know what light your hobbies can put you in. For example, being the member of an amateur dramatics society may not seem like much but will put forward three important skills to your potential employer – a confident individual, a good public speaker, and a person who is comfortable around other individuals.

References

As a finishing touch to your resume, make sure that you have listed at least two references. In some cases, you may be asked for more so it is always better to have some more references that you can call upon at the drop of a hat. While listing their details, include the name, designation, organization name and address, telephone number as well as an email address.

It is advisable that you list your most recent employer as one of your references. If you are anxious about how this would affect your relationship with your current boss in the event that you do not get the job you were applying for, you can always put in a request for the person not to be contacted until your job offer has been secured.

Choosing the Layout and Style

Though this is often regarded as a supplementary aspect of writing a resume, visual aesthetics can go a long way towards being that standout element that sets your application apart from that of your competitors.

Here is a look at the various points that you need to keep in mind while creating the layout and style of your resume if you want it to look professional and stand out at the same time.

Structure and Shape

The shape of a resume defines what impact it is going to have on the reader. Don't forget – hiring managers often have dozens, maybe even hundreds of resumes to go through for a single job posting, so they will not have the time to scrutinize each and every one from top to bottom. A good-looking resume will stand out and catch their eye, inviting them to read on and find out more about you and what your can bring to the company.

The proportion of the page margins is one of the first things that you need to take into account while writing a resume. Standardized margins of 1" are the accepted norm and the safe choice made by as many as 95% of resume writers. While there can be minor variations – which are as small as a tenth of a point – not every amateur writer will be aware of these norms so it is best to stick to something that the industry considers a standard.

This margin specification is also useful for job applicants who lack sufficient experience in writing resumes because this is the largest margin you can have for a resume. Moreover, it gives an impression of your text content being longer than what it actually is.

Length

Just as you have done with the margins, you also need to look at the length of your resume as a critical factor that can have a significant impact on the final aesthetics of your document. It can have enough negative consequences to make it worthy of having some serious consideration. The resume length that can be considered appropriate is another debatable and contentious issue just like the margin.

Alignment

Aligning your resume should be looked upon as a typically straightforward process since every resume is left aligned more often than not. This is the format for reading text ideally followed in western countries. Applicant names and contact details tend to come with center alignment. There are certain style templates where you get these in left aligned form as well.

The resume has certain special segments apart from the contact information area where you can use center alignment in suitable scenarios. The introduction part is also central aligned in some cases. This is something that can be left to personal taste and usually does not have a right or a wrong to how it is done.

Paper Selection

In order to make the perfect resume, selecting the right kind of paper is also very important. The quality of writing should always be given the first priority – every word should be chosen with a purpose and every sentence should have a reason behind its construction. This way you are guaranteed that there can be no better way of writing your resume.

While the content of a resume is undoubtedly important, the spacing, fonts, margins, and formatting also cannot be discounted at any level. Once the completed product is ready, you need to think about printing and distributing the same. This is where the quality of the paper comes into the picture.

Paper Color

Whether you are an amateur or a professional, white is the traditional choice of color for all those writing a resume. It is a neutral color, not contributing or removing anything from the resume pages. This is what has been in use in keeping with traditions and is safe to use irrespective of the career level and industry that you are applying for.

An easy and quick fire way in which you can add a degree of style to your resume is with the use of colored paper. A slightly cream-colored or yellowed document sitting next to a pile of true whites prove to be a standout inclusion while not going overboard as something that is radical or obnoxious. For anyone looking to give their resume a boost and make it stand out in the crowd, this would be a safe option to consider.

Paper Weight, Size and Texture

20 lb. bond paper is the standard weight of papers you see lying around in any office, and also for those being printed through home printers. Though this is an acceptable standard, opting for a slightly more expensive 24-25 lb. bond paper would be more advisable since it is heavier and gives a better feel in the hand. Don't exceed this limit as that will be pushing the limit a little too far, though.

The composition of a paper and the press used in its manufacture helps determine the paper texture. Extremely subtle crosshatching is often used in pressing premium papers while less noticeable imperfections can be observed in others so that they get a unique feel when touched.

A well-weighted paper should be used for printing the resume and it can do without any kind of texture on it. An additional 25% cotton composition would be advisable since it helps in making the paper strong while also adding a feel of crispiness to it. Textured and colored papers are usually manufactured as a premium choice with cotton fiber content of anywhere between 50-100% which makes for an extremely impressive quality of document.

How to Carry Your Resume

You will probably be sending your resume out to several different organizations while applying for a job. Usually, a PDF version is the best choice in such a scenario but it is advisable that you have a look on the job application portal if it is capable of accepting PDF documents.

Sometimes, there are certain portals where you can upload and submit only Word documents and applying with a PDF file here will not be of any kind of use.

Nevertheless, it is important that you have a PDF version of your resume ready with you. While going for an interview, you can also carry it along in a USB thumb drive just in case there is some kind of a contingency situation.

Once you are called to appear for an interview, you need to be present with a printed copy of the resume at the appointment. Of course, you cannot simply walk in with the document dangling in your hand. Some may advise a briefcase but honestly speaking that tends to look a little ungainly and out-of-place.

What you can really do here is invest in a stylish folder to carry your documents and resume in. You will get a vast collection of such folders to choose from. They can also be something tailored to your personality with graphic designs or some other forms of creative artwork.

If you are not used to walking around with a folder in hand, try and get some practice at home. It will be something you need to do right for only a few minutes but that can have a considerable amount of bearing on the overall impression you create in the mind of the employer.

Chapter 25: After The Interview

This can be the most frustrating part of the process as you have completed the interview and now often have no idea whether you will be given the job, asked for a second interview or eliminated from the process for whatever reason. It's not an easy time but there are a few things we can do to make use of our time and prepare us for what might come ahead for us.

The following are a few things everyone should do after any interview. Even when you are told that you are no longer being considered there are benefits to doing each one of these items. After all, no one knows if this same company might have another opening in the near future and you want to be ready to take advantage of it!

Do a Self-Critique or Evaluation

They say hindsight is always 20/20 and by that they mean that after something happens it is easy to see what went right and what went wrong. This applies to interviews as well. Because of this it is important that we take a few moments right after the interview to think about how things went.

As you do this it is important that you are completely honest with yourself. It will not do you much good if you tell yourself you did great when in fact you didn't. No one other than yourself has to hear your thoughts or read your notes. This is strictly for you and you are the one that benefits from the process.

Ask yourself how the interview went overall. Were you calm or nervous? Was the interviewer impressed and positive or did they seem bored or eager to end things early? Did you have good and impressive answers to every question or were there a couple that stumped you or that you didn't have good answers? Did you fall short on anything such as education or specific experience? What do you think the interviewers liked and didn't like about you? What comments did the interviewer make about certain things?

All of this is important because you can use all of this as feedback that will help you do better in a second interview or for the interview for the next job you applied for. This way you learn from your recent interview so you can be more impressive and effective next time.

But be honest with yourself and do this right after the interview. Do not wait a day or a week as some details and information are forgotten over time. Do it while you remember every little detail. Because sometimes it is the little things that can make the biggest difference.

Make Notes About the Interview

As you are doing your self-evaluation or critique, think about what you have learned and write down notes that will help you remember certain things about the interview. Include the questions you either couldn't answer or didn't answer well enough. Write down the high and low points and what the interviewer seemed to like or dislike.

Don't think you will always remember these things because you won't. They will get blurred over time and you need to remember them just like they happened yesterday. Then once you are done, do something with your notes. Correct the little things that you think went wrong. Research those tough questions and come up with better or more effective answers. In other words, turn what are your current interview weaknesses into strengths.

This is very important as it will help you understand what you need to do moving forward. If moving forward means you are getting a second interview, you can use the information in your notes to determine your approach and focus from the last interview. Often you can tell from the questions and the attitude of the interviewer what the company really is looking for or what is more important in the eyes of the company.

Knowing this from the first interview will help you change answers a bit and give them more of what they are looking for. Changing your answers a bit to make them more targeted to what the company wants is a very effective way of making yourself look better and a better match to the position and the company.

If moving forward is an interview for another job in the near future, your notes can help you better prepare and identify weaknesses that need a bit of work. Everyone has them so don't try and fool yourself into thinking you don't. You do have weaknesses and understanding them will help you eliminate them for the next interview.

Send a Follow-Up Thankyou Note

Here is something a lot of applicant don't do and I am not sure why. They are either lazy or just don't think of doing this but it can be one of the smartest things you can do after an interview and it only takes a few minutes to do.

Think about the interviewer for a moment. Chances are they interviewed several other candidates around the same time they interviewed you. Whenever that happens little details are lost and the candidates seem to blur together a bit. So unless you made a super impression that just could not be forgotten you run the risk of the interviewer forgetting which candidate you were. But if you send them a follow-up thank you note thanking them for spending time with you, that can help refresh their memory and bring you and your interview back into focus.

You can also add little details such as how excited you are about the position and maybe a detail or two about relevant experience and education so they remember exactly who you are. If it accomplishes nothing else, writing the letter shows that you are really interested about the position and that this was not just one of 20 interviews you went on this week. Showing that you have passion and interest is never a bad thing.

Prepare for the Next Round Should it Come!

The one thing everyone hopes comes after a first interview is the coveted second interview. This is where the pool of applicants shrinks even further and if you make it to this level, there is definitely interest in you.

As we already recommended, you hopefully have some notes and ideas about how the first interview went. This information can be critical in helping you prepare for the second interview. We will be discussing second and third interviews shortly but for now, let's just say that whatever the first interviewer seemed to focus on should give you a pretty good idea of what they feel is the most important aspects of the job and who they are going to pick to get that job.

Go back and think about what the interviewer said as he described the company and the particular position you are interviewing for. What did they seem to stress about the position and the company? What seemed most important throughout the interview? What did they spend the most time on or ask the most questions about? All of these little bits of information can help you give them more of what they want in the next interview.

Don't sit back and just wait for the next interview. Use that first interview as a building block to help you do even better in the second interview. Doing so will give you a huge advantage over the other applicants who just patted themselves on the back for making it to round two. Don't be one of those applicants. You can pat yourself on the back for making it through but then sit down and use round one to prepare for round two.

Learn from All of Your Interviews

Every interview is a learning experience Whether it is just being exposed and getting comfortable with the different styles of interviews or w just finding out what you were good and not so good in every interview will help you with the next one.

But they will only help you if you let them. Take the time to go back over them. Dissect them and pick them apart. Make a list of good points and not so good points. Then sit down and figure out what you might have done differently or done better.

Acknowledge your performance and take responsibility for it. Do not blame the interviewer or say that they were unfair or didn't know what they were doing. Even though this might be true, it still doesn't help you prepare for next time if you make excuses for this time. When we accept responsibility we learn from our experiences and we get better and become more productive and effective.

Whenever we blame everyone else, we don't change anything. And when nothing is changed, nothing changes.

Remember that after your next interview.

Conclusion

We all know how important interviewing is, and the role it plays in the entire employment process. For many people, the interview is looked upon as the most difficult of all the job-seeking tasks. However, viewing the interview with clouded vision and negative thoughts is a sure fire way to turn the potential "good experience" into a desperately challenging and even negative experience. The way we process and view life is critical to our very presence, and this certainly includes something as important, yet trivial, as an employment interview. The ability to see things in life through clear positive eyes is a reflection of the person you are, and an indication of how you handle things in life, as well as the positive results you achieve.

An interview is indeed a vital part of the overall employment process, but being able to accept the interview and its "sometimes" challenging features, as a mere life experience and certainly a learning experience, should shed some positive light on its potential impact it can have on you as a person. Looking at an interview as an opportunity to meet new people, and perhaps people who can be beneficial to your professional and personal goals, makes the overall experience far more comfortable and even enjoyable. People typically welcome, and take pleasure, in meeting new people and learning about others, and truly the interview process can be looked upon through these very same eyes.

Being able to find inner strength, poise, patience, and know how to venture through the interview process with an open mind, easy heart, confident presence, and playful outlook, makes all the meetings and conversations far less stressful, and even pleasant. Putting aside the professional aspects of an interview, and focusing on the "personal/social" rewards of an interview is a productive approach to the ultimate process. A professional presentation need be present at all times, but certainly, we can line that presentation with smiles, charm, and simple lighthearted conversations as we showcase our skills and professionalism. When our minds are at ease, our bodies relaxed, are presence poised, and our charm ever-present, it is far more enjoyable to go through the rigorous task of interviewing, and come out the other end with feelings of accomplishments in more ways than one.

Remember that everyone, including your recruiter and interviewer, is human and as such will all have an understanding of the various ways that people handle various challenges. With that said many an interviewer keeps light of the fact that candidates are typically nervous when interviewing, and that an interview is not always an accurate depiction of the interviewee. Taking a deep breath and embracing positive thoughts before you begin the long, time-consuming interviewing process, is sure to assist you greatly in answering questions, sharing thoughts, and presenting yourself to your interviewer.

Remember that interviewing is much like a "get acquainted" exercise that allows you and your interviewer to gain an inside look at one another, as well as grasp a genuine understanding of each other. The whole process can be time consuming, yes, but need not be nerve wracking or stressful. The ability to be accepting in life makes everything in life, including interviewing, much easier and more natural. If you can prepare your mindset before entering the interview room to the fact that what is meant to be in life will certainly be, and not over analyze or over rehearse your responses and actions in advance of your meeting, you may be pleasantly surprised at the final outcome. Relaxing your mind is truly the most important element of an interview. By doing so you allow yourself the inner peace and serene atmospheres around you to actually find both interest and enjoyment in the meeting you are about to have. Recognizing that questions warrant answers, and answers should always be truthful and not exaggerated, you will find it much simpler to address the issues that arise, and offer direct honest answers without complication, because you have embraced your own inner peace and willingness to accept the consequences of your presentation, whether good or bad.

It is very easy to lose sight of the big picture when you become obsessed with the simple task of interviewing. The big picture is simply achieving the job you set out to obtain, and joining the team of your potential new company. However, obsessing with the interview itself will have an adverse effect on your overall presence, and your personal presentation. This is exactly what you do not want to happen. You do not want to be so nervous that you fumble over answers, panic, lose direct eye contact, and simply misrepresent yourself. So bottom line is - just relax your mind and body, be honest with your answers, imagine your interview meeting to be a first time meeting of a new friend, and enjoy the experience and all that you will gain from it. What is meant to be in life will always be. Your interview is important yes, but in the end your ability to engage these important new people, and this important interview, with an open mind and ease of heart is more apt to yield results that you are looking for, and ultimately have a pleasant outcome for both candidate and employer.

www.ingramcontent.com/pod-product-compliance
Lightning Source LLC
Chambersburg PA
CBHW072003070526
44583CB00015B/1313